ADMIRALS IN COLLISION

RICHARD HOUGH

Admirals
in Collision

1959

THE VIKING PRESS

NEW YORK

LIBRARY OF CONGRESS CATALOG CARD NUMBER: 59–13415

PRINTED IN THE U.S.A. BY GEORGE MCKIBBIN & SON

ILLUSTRATIONS

ACKNOWLEDGEMENTS

I RECEIVED A GREAT DEAL of information on the officers, the men, and the ships of the Mediterranean Fleet in 1893, from many people—too many to mention each by name, although I am grateful to them all. I should like to thank especially Commander P. K. Kemp, the Admiralty librarian, and his staff; Miss K. Lindsay-MacDougall at the National Maritime Museum, Greenwich; Mr. G. A. Vesey, the Librarian at Bushey, Herts, Public Library, who has so often in the past managed to procure rare and out-of-the-way books, periodicals, and documents. My grateful thanks are also due to Mrs. Iris Penn-Gaskell; Mr. J. David; the Honourable Theodosia Meade, who gave me the photographer of her father, Lord Gillford; Admiral W. Scott-Hill; Captain G. G. P. Hewett, who sent me the photograph of the sinking *Victoria;* Commanders H. P. Mead and W. B. Rowbotham; and Captain James Lumsden, who believes he is the only living survivor of the *Victoria,* who suffered so patiently my questioning, and also found the rare photograph of the *Victoria* firing her guns.

March, 1959   R. H.

AUTHOR'S NOTE

"War," runs the saying, "is nine-tenths boredom and one-tenth hell"; and peace, for a fighting service, has been called ten-tenths boredom. In the closing years of Queen Victoria's reign, the Royal Navy had been at peace for three-quarters of a century, with no more than scattered skirmishes to occupy the time and exercise the theories, initiative, and courage of officers and men. Having grown with Britain's Empire and her responsibilities, the Royal Navy was also the most powerful force in the world, so strong that a single squadron could challenge any other nation's entire navy. Britain's ironclad fleets were the final expression of nineteenth-century power politics, feared abroad as they were loved with a possessive pride at home.

And yet there were some intelligent, far-sighted, and ambitious officers who believed that the years of inactivity threatened to paralyse the Royal Navy's administration, the principles of training, communications, tactics, and ship and weapon design, and so eventually to incapacitate the service as a weapon of war. These officers formed a vocal and powerful minority within the inner councils of the Admiralty. They were mostly regarded as eccentric and a nuisance. They were certainly intelligent, politically influential, and entirely dedicated to their careers—qualities that were essential in order to break down the solidly entrenched traditionalists. But "Jackie" Fisher's massive dreadnought navy of 1914, the only force that could have won or lost World War I "in an afternoon," was the symbol and the actuality of their eventual victory.

This is a book about two admirals who reached flag rank in the early stages of the new generation's struggle for recognition. Both in character and in their service philosophy they were so antagonistic that they almost appear now as destined for explosive fusion. Their paths first crossed in 1888, in the Royal Navy's widely publicized and important naval manœuvres, which began off the Atlantic coast of Ireland, and which provided a unique opportunity for a courageous admiral to justify his unorthodoxy. They concluded in triumph for one and in humiliating defeat for the other. Five years later these same officers met again, in the most dramatic and tragic circumstances, on other manœuvres and on another sea. The causes of the catastrophe that followed are as mysterious, and have been almost as widely debated, as those of the enigma of the *Marie Celeste*.

In this book I have not tried to solve the case of the battleship H.M.S. *Victoria*. I have tried only to show how the strongly contrasting backgrounds, the personalities, and the careers of the two men who were most closely involved in the catastrophe can lead to several possible conclusions. The truth of the *Victoria*, like the truth of the *Marie Celeste* and so many other mysteries of the sea, will never be known.

These, then, are the two admirals whose collision has caused so much controversy in naval circles over the past sixty-six years, as this small selection of comments by authorities reveals:

Vice-Admiral Sir George Tryon, K. C. B.

"It was only the overpowering personality of the man and the confidence he inspired that induced Admiral Markham to carry out an order that was on the face of it insecure."

Admiral of the Fleet Sir Arthur Knyvet Wilson, Bart.

"His brain must have failed him."

Admiral Sir Reginald Bacon

"I believe simply that Sir George Tryon thought he had a much greater power of control over his ships than was really possible."

Rear Admiral Philip H. Colomb

"No one could tell what was in the Admiral's mind beforehand, and Sir George Tryon was not a person who was agreeable on being asked questions or cross-examined."

Admiral Mark Kerr

"Everyone who knew and esteemed the late Sir George Tryon must feel that, though bodily he was present on the afternoon of June 22 last, the guiding brain that made him so dear to us was absent."

Admiral of the Fleet Sir Geoffrey Phipps Hornby

"Have not his countrymen been too hasty in attacking his memory? Is it not possible that they may yet feel ashamed of what they have said or written about him?"

Sir William Laird Clowes

Rear Admiral Albert Hastings Markham

"It is very clear that the Rear Admiral did not understand the signal . . . and went blindly into the danger zone."

Admiral Sir Charles Dundas of Dundas

"If I were Markham . . . I never could hold up my head again."

Admiral of the Fleet Lord Fisher of Kilverstone

"He was crucified alive for another man's blunder."

Admiral Lord Charles Beresford

ADMIRALS IN COLLISION

He conducted his work so skilfully as to prove every
admiral arrayed against him his inferior.

The New York Times

"WAR" WAS OFFICIALLY DECLARED on July 24, 1888.
The enemy's intentions were clear from the start. He would
attempt to break out from his fortified bases with his two
squadrons, cut off Britain's sea communications with the
outside world, and destroy her harbours, ports, and all
other cities within range of his guns.

As the enemy commander-in-chief, Rear Admiral Sir
George Tryon, K.C.B., looked forward with relish to the
task of bringing Britain to her knees. His headquarters
were at Berehaven, in Bantry Bay, on the southwest coast
of Ireland, and his flagship was the ironclad *Hercules,* a
strongly armoured 8000-ton masted battleship armed with
massive 10-inch muzzle-loading guns. Under his command
at Berehaven, Tryon had four more ironclads and cruisers
and supporting light forces; while 250 miles away to the
northeast, at Lough Swilly, he had a further four battleships.

Pitted against Tryon were two British squadrons com-
prising in all thirteen ironclads and an almost overwhelm-
ing number of cruisers, all of which, even before the official declaration of war, had closed in and sealed him in
his two bases. The odds were strongly against Tryon. "The
invading forces can confidently look forward to a resound-

ing defeat should they have the temerity to show themselves beyond the range of their shore-based artillery," was a typical comment reflecting the trust Britain showed in her defending Navy. But Rear Admiral Tryon held certain advantages which were not at once apparent to the uninitiated. Behind the safety of his forts at Berehaven and Lough Swilly, the timing, direction, and method of any break-out were his. He was in constant telegraphic communication by land-line with his second-in-command on the north coast of Ireland. Above all, Tryon was an exceptionally able commander who possessed the imagination and ability to plan his strategy and tactics outside the strictly conservative principles accepted by the Royal Navy.

Tryon had demonstrated his initiative and set the tone of the operation from the beginning by dubbing himself "the Achill Admiral," after a wild and rugged island midway between his bases. It was a name which carried the timbre of victory in its sound, and one which gave him an early moral advantage over his foe. In certain departments of the Admiralty the use of this nickname was regarded as something akin to showmanship and not altogether in the best taste. But even had he known, Sir George would not have been in the least concerned. To him peacetime manœuvres were not a series of games with a strict code of rules and standards of sportsmanship; they were full dress rehearsals for war, realistic and even bitter struggles between the opposing sides. In the war of 1888 he was to make an unorthodox and uncomfortable opponent.

Facing Tryon in this exercise of strength and skill, and in command of the defence of Britain, was Vice-Admiral

John K. E. Baird; but the chief responsibility for keeping the Achill Fleet locked up in its base at Berehaven, rested with Commodore Albert Hastings Markham, who led the inshore squadron of cruisers. It was his task to watch every move of the ships of Tryon's fleet, to close in and attack any that emerged, and hold them in combat until Baird's ironclads could close in for the kill. This was the most responsible command the forty-six-year-old commodore had held, and, in spite of the superiority of the blockading forces, he was not altogether confident that he could carry out his assignment successfully against the formidable Tryon, whose reputation and powerful and colourful personality he found intimidating. With the close presence of Baird's ironclads to support him, the commander of the inshore blockading cruisers could, in theory, hardly fail in his task. But overconfidence was not a fault from which Bertie Markham suffered.

Although it had never been Sir George Tryon's habit to discuss his plans with his subordinates, or even with his staff, he had completed his preparations for war long before Baird's ironclads had heaved to on a chill, choppy ocean off Berehaven, and Markham's cruisers had begun their patrol just outside his base. He would "lie comfortably in harbour, take his own time, create false alarms, worry and harass without serious intent, and finally, when the blockaders were worn out, and sick of the cry of 'Wolf, wolf,' make the actual attempt to break the blockade."[1] By the afternoon of the twenty-fourth, it was "as thick as pea soup and blowing a gale of wind," one correspondent reported; and Tryon contemplated the discomfort of his blockaders with satis-

---

[1] *Life of Vice-Admiral Sir George Tryon, K.C.B.*, by Rear Admiral C. C. Penrose Fitzgerald (1897).

faction. He had been hoping that some really dirty weather would come up to add to the difficulties of Baird and Markham. That night, or perhaps the next, he would send a torpedo boat or two out to keep Markham's nerves on edge. Meanwhile, for the next few days his own officers could relax and enjoy themselves, riding or shooting over the hills of County Cork. "Scarcely a day passed that we did not get ashore for a good walk amongst the beautiful scenery of the Emerald Isle, and wonder why so few ever visit its grand and beautiful west coasts," observed Rear Admiral J. N. East of the *Warspite*, who also found the children "lovely specimens"; although a more jaundiced reporter for *The Times* wrote of the peasantry, "Their cabins are squalid and their habits piggish."

In contrast to Albert Hastings Markham, Sir George Tryon was not inclined to overestimate the power of his opponents; and he certainly had small regard for the commander of the inshore cruisers. He would break the blockade in his own time, link up with his second force on the north coast of Ireland, and from there set about his depredations against British shipping and against the ports of England and Scotland. Victory would not only bring Admiral Tryon the justification of his own daring unorthodoxy; it would raise his personal prestige, bring him even greater publicity, and confirm his position as the most popular and widely admired admiral in the Royal Navy.

For George Tryon was a colourful figure, large and bluff and dynamic, with a dashing, rugged personality that perfectly fitted the public's conception of a bold and aristocratic old salt. Not for eighty years had the British been so eager to love an admiral. If the sentimental, hero-worshipping Victorians could not have another Trafalgar and another Horatio Nelson, at least they could choose for themselves a new naval idol who could be relied upon to thrash the Frogs or deal summarily with the Russian Bear when the time came. Tryon fitted the part perfectly. "He was quite the beau ideal of a sea-dog," wrote one American reporter five years later, "vast of physique and burly, with no poor landsman's reservations about deportment and language, and with a profound and highly vocal contempt for everything not marked down on his own mental chart." The method the Achill Admiral would employ to break out and challenge the blockading ironclads about his base was eagerly awaited by his admirers.

From his first days in the Navy forty years before, the time and the occasion had fallen pat together for Sir George Tryon. It had never been a question of avoiding the wrong turnings, for it seemed as if they had never existed in his career. And now, with the highest honours his service could offer within his grasp, events had shaped themselves to his ambitions. The attention of the whole country was on the Achill Admiral and his men-of-war sheltering in Berehaven harbour. Never before had the annual fleet manœuvres caused such wide interest in Britain. The Royal Navy had gained new prestige from its review the previous year to celebrate Queen Victoria's Golden Jubilee. This great spectacle at Spithead had marked the culminating point in the Royal Navy's struggle for status (and larger appropriations of the taxpayers' money) at the expense of the Army, which had never wholly regained the esteem it had forfeited in the Crimea. The campaign had been set off in 1884 by a series of articles in *The Pall Mall Gazette* entitled "The Truth about the Navy," had continued with public meetings up and down the country addressed by such forceful personalities as Admiral Sir Geoffrey Hornby, and had been supported by a number of newspapers, most vehemently by *The Times*. The cry was always for more money and more men for more ironclads to keep the Empire safe from Britain's potential enemies, and especially from the French, who were becoming dangerously powerful at sea. It was more successful than its promoters could have hoped for. By 1888 a new programme of construction was in hand; and "Jack Tar" had become to the nation a sentimental figure symbolizing the security of Britain's far-flung possessions, and the black ironclad a romantic expression of the nation's jingoism. The country now felt a strong sense of possession toward its men-of-war; the Navy was "Our Navy"—it belonged to the Queen and her people, who followed with pride every detail about its men, its ships, and their activities.

One of the revolutionary steps the Sea Lords of the Admiralty had taken in their campaign was to encourage the appointment by newspapers of naval correspondents, and even to allow them on board during manœuvres. The 1888 manœuvres provided these correspondents with a golden opportunity to prove themselves, and they were all given column after column, days before war was declared, to explain the order of battle to their readers, to describe the senior officers taking part and the ships in which they served, and the tasks which the two sides had been set. For the purpose of the manœuvres, readers were told, Ireland was presumed to be an enemy country with a powerful battle fleet, but one inferior in strength to Britain's. To all but the most naïve, of course, Ireland represented France, whose fleet was about to leave to attack Britain and to prepare the way for a landing by her more powerful army. But the fleet's departure was anticipated by the declaration of war and the arrival off its bases of blockading squadrons.

The whole nation identified itself with this game of mock-warfare as if it were a new form of sport put on for its benefit. Would the nonconformist, hard-hitting George Tryon succeed in breaking through the blockade? And if he did, would he stand any sort of chance against the formidable fleets awaiting his appearance? "All is excitement," reported *The Times* correspondent on board the *Ajax* at Berehaven on the day hostilities began, "and yet this is only the very beginning of the play." *The Times* correspondent had already described in detail the five-mile-long harbour at Berehaven, formed between Bere Island and the mainland, its two entrances at its western and eastern ends, its Martello towers and its other defensive features: its ships' guns ashore, the wire hawsers strung across the entrances as protection against torpedo attack, its searchlights that swept the water constantly at night. Along this rugged coastline, just three hundred years before, some of the remnants of the greatest armada that had ever attempted an invasion of Britain had run ashore and been wrecked. Now the country was to be shown whether, under a similar threat, Britain could survive. It was an intriguing fantasy that was followed with great attention. Could the Navy beat off her enemies as she had in 1588? Were the ironclads of today the equal of the *Revenge* and the *Victory?* Above all, were Baird and Markham as bold, determined, and capable as Drake and Hawkins had shown themselves three hundred years before? Rear Admiral Sir George Tryon was to prove that they were not.

On the evening of the first day of hostilities, Tryon set off the first of his false alarms, and Markham's cruisers, patrolling in a gale close inshore, sent up rocket signals to Admiral Baird indicating that two torpedo boats and a battleship were escaping. During the next two days Tryon was content to watch the tossing dark shapes of Baird's ironclads on the skyline from the peaceful security of his anchorage, while his shore batteries loosed off a few blank rounds from time to time at Markham when he ventured in too close to them. On the fourth evening Tryon opened up the defence barriers across the western entrance and sent two of his torpedo boats out under cover of darkness and with all lights obscured. The intention of the foray was to keep Markham's nerves on edge and set off more false alarms. But the two little boats did better than that; just before dawn they returned in triumph with four enemy torpedo boats which they had stalked, surprised, and captured almost under the cliffs of Black Ball Head.

By August 2, George Tryon decided that there had been enough of this teasing and that it was time for action. To be tossed about for nine days and nights in a state of alternating alarm and boredom was enough to tax the patience and good humour of the hardiest bluejacket, and he knew that the enemy's morale must be as low as the coal in their vessels' bunkers. By 6 p.m. on August 3 the whole of the Achill Fleet had steam up, the upper works and boats of their ships had been painted black, and every commander had been issued with his secret orders. At 9:30 everything was ready, and, as darkness fell, Tryon's fastest vessels—the *Warspite, Iris, Severn, Volage,* and *Cossack,* and three torpedo boats—crept out through the western entrance, and, hugging dangerously close to the cliffs, proceeded

towards Dursey Head and the Atlantic. Simultaneously
Tryon emerged with deliberate, but not too flagrant, in
discretion from the eastern entrance, and made as if to
break through the defensive cordon. Within an hour Markham's searchlights had picked up the *Hercules* and her companions, and at once fierce excitement broke out among the
blockading vessels, with flares and Very lights and searchlights flashing in every direction—"an indescribably beautiful and exciting scene," one correspondent cabled home.

When he saw Markham's ships cutting through the water
towards him, Tryon turned round through 180 degrees and
hastened back towards Berehaven at full speed, narrowly
missing being torpedoed on the way by his pursuers. As the
Hercules heaved to and dropped anchor behind the shelter
of Bere Island and its fortresses, more flares were arching up
above the cliffs to the west, showing that the *Warspite* and
her companions had been discovered at last by the only ship
that had not been drawn off its patrol line by Tryon's
stratagem.

Tryon's last deception had worked perfectly, and it was
not until well into the next day that Baird and Markham
realized that the *Warspite* and the other swift and powerful
enemy ships had escaped into the Atlantic before dawn.
What was the cause of this débâcle for the blockaders?
wrote Rear Admiral J. N. East exultantly aboard the flee-
ing *Warspite*. Was the blockaders' "universally popular and
gallant Admiral entertaining his captains at his hospitable
table, and cracking jokes about 'dear George's bounce'?"

There was only one counter-move Baird could make now,
and that was to raise immediately the blockade at Berehaven, and also at Lough Swilly to the north, and somehow
try to prevent the Achill Fleet from reaching the shores of

England and Scotland. This was a hopeless task from the start. Tryon had worked out his plans to the last detail with his second-in-command, Rear Admiral Charles J. Rowley. As soon as he received news from his lookouts posted on Bere Island that Markham and Baird were leaving, he prepared for sea again, and that night he sailed in the *Hercules* with the remainder of his fleet for Lough Swilly to join up with the slower ships of Rowley's detachment.

And now George Tryon proceeded to demonstrate the damage that could be caused to British shipping, and how the coastal towns and cities could be devastated and their life brought to a standstill, by a series of scattered, swift, and well-coordinated attacks from an enemy fleet. It was true that several of his subordinates got rather out of hand, that crack Atlantic liners were "sunk" by 13-knot cruisers, that large towns were "wiped out" by lightly armed torpedo boats without warning. But to Tryon this was war, not a polite exercise, and he had instilled into his captains the need for enthusiasm and realism. "With regard to the bombardment of defenceless towns and the destruction of private property, as impossible amongst civilized nations," wrote one of Tryon's officers in his defence later, "I commend to their [his critics'] notice the signal which was made by Sir Charles Napier in the Baltic directly after war was declared with Russia in 1854: 'Sink, burn, and destroy everything Russian.' " Tryon and his commanders certainly showed ruthlessness as well as devastating efficiency. "Steamers and small sailing vessels were captured and destroyed as they came within range," one of his detachments reported as it swept through the Pentland Firth at

12 knots. "We could not stop to pick up their crews, but trust they escaped in their boats."

Tryon's fastest ships proceeded round the north coast of Scotland and set about the eastern coastal towns and harbours. At Aberdeen all shipping was sunk in half an hour and £400,000 levied from the population. "The afternoon of the same day found us steaming up the Forth, carrying havoc on both sides of its lovely shores. The Forth bridge was destroyed at about 4 o'clock, and Edinburgh refusing the modest indemnity of one million pounds demanded of her, the modern Athens was left in flames." Shields produced half a million, Newcastle a million, after heavy bombardment. "There was no protection of any kind for the enormous wealth of Great Grimsby and Hull," reported Admiral East from the *Warspite*. Grimsby was therefore laid in ashes, and "a pilot whom we beckoned alongside informed us that the English Ministry had been impeached for high treason, and the Sea Lords of the Admiralty shot by an indignant people."

After joining up with three of Rowley's ironclads, Tryon led the rest of the Achill Fleet across the Irish Sea to Liverpool. A defending squadron had just left the city, and Tryon dealt summarily with the obsolete old guns of the fortress, captured an enemy ironclad, and steamed up the Mersey, to the enormous excitement of the local population. A great crowd poured down to the landing-stages and pierheads to watch the bombardment of their city, and soon the great guns of the *Hercules, Hero, Ajax, Invincible,* and *Devastation* opened up a thundering barrage of blank shells. With the destruction completed, Tryon sent a "hospitable dispatch" to the Lord Mayor. In view of the "really generous

welcome and hospitalities that Liverpool had always extended to the seamen of all nations," he wrote, "I will only
demand for the moment that his Worship and his successors should be compelled, if asked, to dine with the Admiral
and his successors at least once a year. . . ."

It was astute of George Tryon to complete his sweeping
victory on a light note. For by the time the re-formed
squadrons of the Achill Fleet were steaming up Channel
for London, when peace was declared, the cries of protest
from the commanders of the bewildered, scattered squadrons of the defending forces were already being heard,
claiming that Tryon's methods had been unfair and not in
accordance with the rules. Merchant ships could not be
destroyed without giving due warning to their crews and
time for boats to be launched. Nor was it customary for
defenceless cities to be bombarded and innocent civilians to
be killed. There had been talk of Achill men-of-war dis-
playing the wrong flags and using captured enemy telegraphic equipment. George Tryon had gone too far this
time, ran the bitter comment in the wardrooms of Baird's
and Markham's defeated vessels. It just wasn't cricket.

But to his many admirers among the ordinary people
Tryon's dramatic breaking of the blockade, and the swift
and pulverizing attacks on Glasgow and Edinburgh, Newcastle, and Hull, and a dozen other ports that had followed,
appeared in perfect character with his heroic and dashing
personality; and they appeared to take a perverse delight
in the knowledge that their country was so vulnerable to
attack by an inferior force.

"Oh, I like manœuvres because they wake the Admiralty
up," Tryon remarked to a fellow officer at the conclusion
of the 1888 exercises. And the Sea Lords themselves were

well satisfied. Tryon could be relied upon to do the right thing, and as the official report stated: "The main lesson which these manœuvres emphasize is that Great Britain, whose maritime supply is her life, is very far from being as strong as she should be on the seas. . . . The defeat of her Navy means to her the loss of India and her colonies, and her place among the nations." The sortie from Berehaven had been "admirably contrived"; and they considered that he had acted with skill and promptitude in his assaults on the English and Scottish coasts. For the following year the Naval Estimates were substantially increased. For Sir George Tryon even greater honours in the Royal Navy lay ahead.

It was comforting for the British people to know that George Tryon was "really on our side." While the Navy possessed officers of his calibre, Britannia could still rule the waves. But there was no comfort in the result for the commanders of the defending forces, some of whom in the past had seen the admiral promoted over their heads and, when serving under him on other exercises, had suffered from his unpredictable methods and his scathing comments. As one correspondent wrote of the 1888 manœuvres: "His rapid movements and ceaseless energy were a constant theme of admiration among naval critics. To such an extent did his results disparage his opponents that several of them were regarded for a time as under the severe displeasure of the Admiralty." Among these was the officer most responsible for the escape from Berehaven of the Achill Admiral, Commodore Albert Hastings Markham.

His was a fine character, and he never showed that better than in the days which brought him so much sadness.

Admiral of the Fleet Earl Jellicoe

IT WAS ONLY BY A STROKE of good fortune that Albert Markham had got into the Navy at all, after failing to obtain nomination before he had passed the statutory age limit. It had been particularly important for young Bertie to find employment and stand on his own feet as soon as possible, as he was the fifth son to be born within five years, and his family, already desperately short of money, could not afford to continue his education on their own resources. Just as his father had given up in despair of ever finding anyone influential enough to provide the necessary nomination, the Admiralty tried the short-lived experiment of accepting cadets over the age of fourteen years, and in the spring of 1855 the father succeeded at last in finding a nominator for his son. A few weeks later Bertie passed his preparatory cadetship examination.

Albert Hastings Markham was born at Bagnères-de-Bigorre in the Pyrenees on November 11, 1841, just two days after a more famous Bertie, later King Edward VII, whom he was so closely to resemble in later life. His paternal grandfather was Dr. William Markham, Archbishop of York, and his father, John, had retired from the Navy himself because of ill health, with the rank of lieutenant, many years before, and had since lived mainly on his inadequate capital. The family's spirit was dominated by a stoic acceptance of their poverty during Bertie's infancy in France and later when they moved to Guernsey to try their hand at farming. Life was austere, the daily round rigid, severe, and devout. There was little of childhood frivolity for Bertie, and a sense of duty and a sense of dour righteousness were the most apparent characteristics he had acquired when he was sent to London at the age of thirteen to prepare himself for the Royal Navy.

Bertie's home in London was with an aunt, the widow of his father's brother, the late Reverend David Markham, Canon of Windsor. There he met for the first time the young man who was to become the strongest influence in his life, and whom he was to come to admire almost to the point of idolatry. This was his cousin Clements Markham, who responded with warmth to Bertie's admiration and at once accepted him as an equal in spite of the eleven years between their ages. Clements, an edgy, energetic, and emotional man, served briefly in the Royal Navy himself, was to be knighted for his work in exploration, and was to become the most famous geographer of his day; it was he who selected Scott for the first of the Antarctic Expeditions fifty years later. He instilled into his young cousin an early interest in geography, in natural history and the sciences, and in writing, during the period they lived together at 4 Onslow Square, where, appropriately enough, their neighbours were Admiral Fitzroy, the distinguished naval scientist, and Thackeray, who passed the window every morning at breakfast time.

The most obvious and striking contrast between Clements and Bertie Markham, who had so much else in common, was revealed by their reaction to naval life. Clements served in all for seven years, found it distasteful and uncongenial, and would not have retained his commission for so long had he not seen the opportunity of taking part in the Sir John Franklin search expedition. He disliked the restrictions on his freedom and on the expression of his individuality that the service imposed, and was by nature too impatient to await the slow rise to seniority that would allow him the initiative and responsibility to which he believed he was entitled. Clements was a born organizer and supervisor, and these qualities, he always felt, well merited the admiration of those satellites by whom he liked to be surrounded. For more than fifty years the brightest-glowing twin satellites, and the most unwavering in their orbit about him, were his wife Minna and his cousin Bertie.

Life in the Royal Navy was at first equally uncongenial to Albert Markham. He had expressed no particular wish to join in the first place, although, as always, he was ready to follow the directions and advice of his elders and betters. But, except for periods of half-pay, he remained loyal to the service for fifty-one years. Like his cousin, he was miserably seasick, suffered under a stern tutor when preparing for his entry examination and under an ill-tempered martinet on his first ship. He hated having to watch the public floggings on H.M.S. *Victory* at Portsmouth, and the many cruelties of a service in which conditions were little different from those that had existed at the time of the Nore Mutiny. He was never a dedicated career officer, and, like his cousin, resented the demands and restrictions the service forced on him. But the stern austerity of his upbringing had prepared him for severer trials than the more wayward Clements was ready to tolerate, and he bore his resentments in silence. Besides, Bertie had his living to earn.

At fourteen Albert Markham was sent out East on the sloop *Camilla,* and there saw eventful active service. He arrived in Hong Kong in 1856 to find many members of the English colony, among them his brother John whom he had not seen for eight years, suffering from food poisoning, caused by arsenic put in the flour by ill-disposed Chinese. This was not considered an exceptional ordeal by the guardians of the Empire in that remote region, and it was commonplace for pirate junks to make tip-and-run raids on Hong Kong harbour shipping at the time. For the next three years Bertie's time was mostly occupied with patrols and forays against these pirates, whose cruelty and cunning provided such excellent material for authors of Victorian boys' fiction. Between punitive expeditions, a British Consulate official at Amoy, who temporarily claimed Bertie's easy devotion, helped to stimulate his natural interest in ornithology, and Bertie shot almost as many snipe among the paddy fields as he shot pirates among the river estuaries. But he also proved himself a brave cadet, and later a bold midshipman, for the odds were not always in favour of the Royal Navy. He was still only fifteen when he led six boys and a couple of Marines in a jolly-boat against a pirate junk. When the pirates began leaping overboard at the attack, his boat picked up a number of them and took them back to be beheaded by the local mandarin. On another occasion he took a lorcha, armed with a camouflaged 12-pounder howitzer, against a pirate vessel suspected of holding captive two British subjects. This incident led to a three-hour bloody fight, and Markham took five men in a sampan and attempted to board the pirate vessel, outnumbered ten to one. He was at first driven off, but finally succeeded in climbing aboard under heavy fire, and took eleven pirates prisoner in hand-to-hand combat. The British captives, they found when they went below, had already been crucified, and the pirates were accordingly executed.

Bertie became involved in numerous skirmishes, ashore and afloat, in China and later in Japan, before he returned home in 1864 to a warm welcome from Clements and Minna. He stayed with them in their London house, which for thirty years was his only home, took his lieutenant's examination nine months later, and left in November for service in the Mediterranean on board the last three-decker to be commissioned in the Royal Navy, H.M.S. *Victoria*. The next three years were less spartan, less uncongenial, and much less dangerous. In the Levant, on the rare occasions of local disorder, to show the flag was always sufficient, and the might and influence of Britain were undisputed. It was a leisurely life that allowed plenty of time for recreation ashore, and Bertie Markham took full advantage of this to explore the ruins and treasures of Italy and Turkey, the Holy Land, Egypt and Greece and the Aegean Islands. To many officers a "mopping up of the Levant," as it was colloquially termed, was something of a tedious chore compared with the delights of a cruise along the Italian and French Rivieras. But to the studious and earnest Lieutenant Albert Markham it provided a wonderful opportunity at last to discover for himself the riches of ancient civilizations, as well as the natural history and the geography of a new region of which he had heard so much from Clements. He recorded his impressions in a journal which he kept throughout his naval career. If the observations sometimes lacked profundity and originality, and the style was over-elaborate to the point of dullness, he never missed an entry, and his handwriting, like everything about him, was always meticulously neat. During his Mediterranean tour of duty, he was often able to meet Minna and his cousin ashore; and his two greatest pleasures were to travel on archaeological expeditions with them, learning at first hand from his beloved Clements, and to read aloud to them the entries in his journal since their last meeting, perhaps receiving from time to time some word of praise for his keen observation.

Together, the restless Clements and his gentle, adoring wife provided the nucleus of Bertie's life. They were his home and family, his stimulus, his relaxation. They talked his language, understood his frustrations, sympathized, encouraged, and cultivated his mind. Away from them he was often moody, irritable, and defensive, resenting his naval career the more because his sense of duty, as well as his need of the pay, demanded that his loyalty to the service should be uncompromising. This moral dutifulness, supported by his strong and almost puritanical religious convictions, led to conflicts which made him a difficult fellow officer in the wardroom. He neither smoked nor drank, and was always ready to express his disapproval of those indulgences. Later, when he reached senior rank, he was often a domineering commander, and once lectured his officers: "A gentleman may be forgiven an occasional cigar, cigarettes are only for effeminate weaklings, but the low, filthy, and nauseous black pipe can only be compared with gin and other disreputable liquors which ruin mind and body."

On watch, on manœuvres or exercises, or at gunnery drill, Albert Markham devoted himself wholly to his duties. He followed authorized and established practice, he was a good seaman, punctilious in his conduct and correct in his adherence to naval discipline. It was clear he would go far. But he did not conceal from Clements and Minna his distaste for the tedious routine of peacetime service life, with its cruises and elaborate ritual and time-wasting panoply. The wardroom junketings, the meaningless frivolity of shipboard entertainment and balls, the self-indulgent and worthless parties ashore, were all alien to his severe moral fastidiousness.

Early in 1868 he was sent out to the Australian station as First Lieutenant of H.M.S. *Blanche,* and he found greater purpose in service in the Pacific, putting down the slave traffic between Queensland and the South Sea islands. This was much more to his taste, although he sadly missed the comfort of Clements' and Minna's proximity, and he soon became involved in a difficult political conflict. He was to discover that it was not simply a question of preventing slave traders from "blackbirding" natives to the Queensland cotton plantations. Some of the natives welcomed the idea, others hated any white men, slavers and anti-slavers alike, and the colonial government was not so sympathetic towards the stamping out of the traffic as it might have been. Markham succeeded in making himself equally unpopular among all parties involved by intercepting numerous slave ships, returning home their cargoes, and fighting punitive actions against a certain tribe on the island of Nakapa in the Swallow Group north of Santa Cruz, which had murdered a bishop and three other whites. Markham landed without hesitation amidst a cloud of poisoned arrows, drove the natives from their village, set fire to their huts, destroyed their canoes, and departed. It was one thing to defend helpless blacks from unscrupulous profiteers; but when these same blacks responded to the word of God by killing servants of the Church, drastic action was called for. On his return to England soon after this incident, he discovered that there had been strong criticism of his apparent cruelty in both Houses of Parliament and in the press.[1]

But the Sea Lords of the Admiralty were impressed by the decisiveness and energy he had shown during this commission, and disregarded the public criticism of his action at Nakapa. In the spring of 1872 Albert Markham was promoted to the rank of commander.

While he was still a young man, Markham's family had emigrated to the United States in a last effort to recoup their fortunes, and John Markham had bought a farm near La Crosse in Wisconsin. Bertie visited them twice, once before and once after his father's death, and he recorded, in his usual flat style, his experiences on his journeys. This narrative revealed his irritability at the slow trains ("I have now travelled over 1000 miles and have seldom done more than 24 m.p.h."); his disgust at the hotels, where the swearing, spitting, and drinking shocked him deeply; his concern at the transparently murderous character of some of his fellow travellers on a stagecoach to Dodge City—a town which he found too fast and too noisy for his taste. He was, however, much impressed by the beauty of the scenery, the richness of the wildlife in the Mississippi Valley, and "the remarkable wooden buildings" of Chicago. On his second trip, in 1877, he was invited on a grand hunting expedition through Indian territory along Red River.

[1] Before leaving the Pacific, Markham chanced to be asked for his advice on the design of a flag for the new New Zealand Marine. "You have already the right to fly the Blue Ensign," Markham suggested. "Why not add to it the stars of the Southern Cross?"

He set out with his host, a General Mackenzie, in a large wagon, accompanied by a sergeant, two corporals, twelve troopers, three cavalry officers, two teamsters, a personal servant, and five greyhounds. The sport was rich—buffalo, elk, deer, antelope, wild turkey, duck, teal, and quail—and he described the killings in his journal with the usual satisfied relish he reserved for his hunting exploits. Wherever he travelled, Bertie Markham killed. To him, as to so many of his contemporary natural historians, the study and the slaughter of wildlife were synonymous. Only the destruction and subsequent flensing of whales, which he witnessed on his later Arctic voyages, appeared to affect him, and he owned to "a never-failing sense of repugnance in watching the dying struggles of the unfortunate monsters."

Markham's first interest in Arctic exploration had been fired by Clements when he was still serving as a lieutenant in the Mediterranean, and in subsequent years the unexplored Arctic wastes developed an irresistible fascination for him. Clements encouraged him to read everything that was known about the region and about the early explorers, such as Ross and Franklin, and told him all that he knew himself from his own journeys. After the Admiralty refused to make use of his services officially, Bertie at length determined to go on his own account when he could afford to. He had not the means to commission an expedition, nor could he find the money to sail as a passenger; so in the end he resolved to apply for leave and sign on as a crew member of a whaler. He made two such trips, once as second mate in the whaler *Arctic* to Greenland and the Davis Straits, and later in a Norwegian cutter to Novaya Zemlya. It required courage to submit to the rigours of the quarters on a whaler after the luxuries of Royal Navy wardrooms, but Bertie confessed to being more deeply shocked by the language and drunkenness than by the discomforts and coarse food. The whaler fleet's captains would meet from time to time on board the *Arctic* for a "mollie," which was nothing less than an all-night binge. Bertie kept well clear of these, though he wrote that he "found his conversation with some of the skippers most interesting"—presumably in the earlier stages of a mollie. On the Norwegian ship it was the lack of seamanship that offended him as deeply as the inebriation, and the captain, "a very old man and very fond of the bottle," rarely appeared from his cabin, and was "totally unacquainted with the mysteries of navigation." Even old liquor barrels were used for the storage of the fresh water, which, to Bertie's disgust, both smelled and tasted of rum. But, besides some of the raw aspects of life at sea, Markham learned a great deal on the whaling trip that was to be invaluable to him three years later, and the shores of Novya Zemlya provided him with the most exciting opportunity in his life for the study of the rarer breeds of northern birds, such as the Arctic tern and the pomatorhine skua.

Albert Markham's life was clearly divided into three parts by his successful Arctic expedition of 1875–76 and the tragic event of 1893; and by the fame he enjoyed as a result of the first and the distress he suffered from the second. In the early summer of 1875 an official Naval Expedition, under Captain George S. Nares, left Plymouth to explore the Far North. Markham had been given the command of one of the three vessels forming the expedition, and was appointed to lead the northern party, whose aim was to continue by boat and sledge to explore the farthest regions and record details of the geography and physical conditions close to the Pole. Markham's last letter to Clements and Minna had suggested it would be "rather nice to have prayers said for our expedition"; and before his return eighteen months later he had had need of all the spiritual support his cousin and the congregation of the local church could offer.

The winter was a particularly hard one and the cold in the frozen-up ships was bitter (although Bertie strongly disapproved of the extra issue of grog authorized for the men by Nares); and when the northern party under his command finally got away with the reappearance of the sun in February, everything went wrong. Markham had unfortunately omitted to take a ration of lime juice for his party, and before they had got far, one-third of the men had been stricken with scurvy. Eleven of the party eventually were unable to walk, and one died in Markham's arms. In spite of the appalling hardships, the survivors dragged the sick members by sledge over palaeocrystic ice and snow to within 399½ miles of the Pole, the farthest north any man had ever reached. Markham staged a small celebration of the event, with three cheers and a chorus from "The Union Jack of Old England." And then they set off back to base, with Markham reading aloud from Scott's *The Pirate* to keep up the spirits of the men. On June 14 the depleted party were helped back over the last miles and given a triumphant welcome by Nares and the rest of the expedition. In London in November Markham received a gold watch from the Royal Geographical Society and was promoted to the rank of captain. But it was the esteem of Clements and the warmth of the reception from Minna that gave Bertie Markham the greatest pleasure. Later he wrote a book about the expedition and called it *The Great Frozen North*.

Albert Markham's subsequent naval career was more orthodox. He would dearly have liked to take extended periods of leave in order to continue his geographical research, to write books and spend more of his time with Clements, but, unlike so many of his fellow officers, he had no private means. He was still a bachelor. The one woman of any consequence in his life was Minna, for whom he held only a warm, brotherly affection; and at thirty-five the only passion that he revealed to his intimates was for a deeper knowledge of the geography, history, and natural life of the world. He showed little interest in his fellow men, and his service relationships were tenuous and lacked intimacy. Away from the warm comfort of Clements and Minna—in the Channel Squadron, as flag captain to the commander-in-chief of the Pacific Station, in the West Indies and the Baltic—he was acquiring a reputation as a prickly, obstinate, and unsociable officer, almost as a recluse because he would remain in his cabin for long periods writing his journal, letters to Clements, one of his books about the Arctic and its explorers, or one of his uplifting contributions to *Good Words*. As captain of the battleship *Triumph*, which was in a poor state of morale when he assumed command at Callao in 1879, he dealt harshly with drunkenness and indiscipline and stopped all leave. "I wonder," he wrote unhappily in his journal, "if the men have any idea that I feel the punishment I inflict upon them as much as they do themselves."

By 1891 Markham was at the top of the captain's list, and in the normal course of promotion would soon acquire flag rank. In the Admiralty he was regarded without special favour or disfavour, but in spite of small lapses (such as the escape of the Achill Fleet from Berehaven), as a competent and steady officer. He would, the Sea Lords considered, make an admirable second-in-command to the brilliant and forceful new commander of the Royal Navy's premier squadron. In January 1892 Albert Hastings Markham was appointed Rear Admiral to Vice-Admiral Sir George Tryon, K.C.B., Commander-in-Chief of the Mediterranean Fleet.

Most people felt no use arguing with George Tryon, and that it was better to acquiesce quietly . . . the art of persuasion without seeming to persuade was one of his strong points.

Rear Admiral C. C. Penrose Fitzgerald

GEORGE TRYON REGARDED HIS APPOINTMENT to the senior seagoing command in the world's greatest navy as no more than entitlement, a merited and even preordained promotion in a career which a fellow officer,[1] who bore him no special love, described as one which "he had laid out before him from his earliest days." He was a member of that privileged class who succeeded, all within the life-span of one remarkable woman, in cultivating the advantages accorded by their birth, receiving their due distinctions, and dying honoured by a society they had enriched. In his biography of Tryon, which is sometimes refreshingly astringent, Rear Admiral C. C. Penrose Fitzgerald wrote: "It is perhaps no great compliment to say that Tryon never showed jealousy of any of his brother officers, for it may pertinently be replied that he never had occasion for it." And even his service contemporaries said of George Tryon that he never took a false step until the one that destroyed him.

George Tryon was born on January 4, 1832, the third

[1] Captain P. H. Colomb, R.N., writing in the *Saturday Review*, February 27, 1897.

son of Thomas Tryon of Bulwick Park, Northamptonshire, and Ann, daughter of Sir John Trollope, Bart. His family was rich, his father successful and influential, his home background happy and secure. He enjoyed every moment of his time at Eton. "There never was such a nice place as it," he wrote later, "and there never will be"; he also found it "a letter of introduction to the best kind all over the world." His two elder brothers, Tom and Henry, and his younger brother Richard all chose the Army as a career and served with honour at Alma and Inkerman and in the Indian Mutiny. But George, at the late age of sixteen, suddenly announced to his father that he wished to join the Navy. He had none of the difficulties of Albert Markham in obtaining nomination, Thomas Tryon saw to that, and in the early spring of 1848 he passed his entry examination and joined H.M.S. *Wellesley* at Plymouth. His late entry into the service proved no disadvantage. "On the contrary," wrote Fitzgerald, "his public school training gave him a greater breadth of view and made him a quicker and readier learner, than many of his contemporaries, who had joined the Navy some years younger."

No naval cadet in the mid-nineteenth century had a soft or easy time. But George Tryon's training period was a great deal less rigorous than Markham's on the China Station was to be. The *Wellesley* was attached to the North American Squadron, and after passing—comfortably in top place—his midshipman's examination, he was taken up and shown special favours (such as the use of his cabin) by Lieutenant Cochrane, the son of the Commander-in-Chief, the Earl of Dundonald. While life for Markham was sometimes made miserable on the East Indies Station by his commander, and he was once demoted for failing on watch to ensure that "All's well" was called, Tryon thrived in the West Indies, "the captain and commander taking him up too, and he was very soon given charge of a boat."

At eighteen, Tryon was a tall midshipman with broad shoulders, curly brown hair, and a cupid's-bow mouth—dashingly handsome in his epaulettes and tight-fitting uniform, supremely conscious of the privileges life had bestowed on him, and confident of his ability to promote them to the advantage of his career and the service. He was socially at ease in any company, showed appropriate respect to his superiors, and accepted with pleasure and apparent modesty the admiration that so often came his way. He was high-spirited and an initiator of gunroom larks, but studious and conscientious at his lessons and on watch. He wrote long and rambling letters to his mother (he was, later, equally devoted to his mother-in-law), describing the wonders of the New World—beach picnics at Bermuda, shooting ashore, sailing in the Caribbean, high jinks at the tough little port of Halifax, where "the other day another of our men was murdered, beaten with sticks to death. So our men when on leave attacked the house he was found in, beat all the occupants, and burned it to the ground." In the United States he found it remarkable that there were no beggars. "We have not seen one, and only heard two organs. There was no lean horses, and no starving dogs, and the Irishmen seem well contented." This was not at all as he had imagined a foreign country; and the United States even had a form of self-government, of a crude kind, he discovered in Washington, where he was introduced to the leading statesmen of the day. One difference between the Senate and the House of Representatives, he explained to his mother, is "in the latter they blackguard each other in the highest terms, and in the former they are at all events tolerably civil to one another." The debate he listened to from the strangers' gallery, he wrote, "was most interesting. It was concerning the admission of California, which State wishes to be admitted as a free state, not as a slave state. The Northern States, who have no slaves, have no need for them, and are for the abolition of slavery. The Southern men, again, are all for slavery; for they would be ruined if slavery was abolished. . . . The Northerners preach about the horrors of slavery, &c., &c.—in fact have quite the same opinion as Englishmen; for they can afford to be magnanimous at the expense of their neighbours. . . . It is a very difficult question to settle, especially as the Southern States say they will separate themselves from the Union if slavery is abolished, and there is little doubt but that they will."

In June 1851 the *Wellesley* returned home and paid off at Chatham. For Tryon it had been a highly successful commission, and he had enjoyed every moment of it.

Three years later, on the southern shores of the Black Sea, Tryon was making a sketch of the wrecked Turkish fleet after the massacre of Sinop. "We are all so annoyed about it," he wrote home; and within eight months he was watching the Battle of the Alma from the maintop of H.M.S. *Vengeance* through a glass, reporting progress to those below. "At about eleven the army was seen to advance; the French and Turks close to the shore, climbed up a very steep road, which the Russians were unable to prevent, as our guns would have knocked them over. The French rushed up most gallantly; the artillery had a tremendous drag to get up at all; twice we saw the French shelter under the brow of the hill, making a short retreat

from the murderous fire. . . ." Tryon joined the Naval
Brigade after Inkerman, fought at the siege of Sevastopol
with two of his brothers, helped bury Henry, and saw Tom
invalided home sick.

At the end of the Crimean War, Tryon was a lieutenant,
with honourable wounds, highly regarded by his immediate seniors, a favourite in any wardroom. "But it must
have been obvious to him," Fitzgerald wrote, "that unless
he could get some special appointment, such as a flag
lieutenancy on the royal yacht, so as to carry him over the
heads of many of his seniors, there would be very little
chance of his being in the first flight of his profession, and
reaching the highest ranks; and nothing less than this
would satisfy his ambition." Once again, his ambition was
to be satisfied: Her Majesty selected him from the numerous
applicants for royal yacht service, which gave him automatic
promotion to the rank of commander within two years. "It
must be admitted that Tryon was lucky," Fitzgerald wryly
observed; and at the end of the two years the *Royal Albert's*
captain described him "as an officer of great zeal and
promise. His ready resource, active intelligence, sound
judgement and good temper, especially qualify him for
success in his profession. . . ."

H.M.S. *Warrior* was as revolutionary a ship, as important a vessel in the history of naval design, as the *Dreadnought* half a century, or the *Nautilus* a century, later. In
1850 the battleship had not changed basically for hundreds
of years. She had the same general shape, the same rig, the
same tiers of smooth-bore guns, as the vessels that had
fought at the Nile and the Boyne. But with the coming of
the shells and of steam all this was to be changed—first by
the French with *La Gloire* in 1858, and, in alarmed reply to

this in Britain, by Scott Russell's *Warrior,* the first true seagoing ironclad in the Royal Navy. At the time of her commissioning she was the most beautiful, most publicized and highly regarded vessel in the service: the Royal Navy's crack ship, unique with her armour-plated hull, huge 1250-horsepower engine, and speed of fourteen knots. The *Warrior* made every other ship of the line obsolete, and every officer would have dropped a rank to serve on her. In October 1861, George Tryon was appointed her commander.

Tryon's service on the *Warrior* established his reputation with the Admiralty as one of the most promising commanders in the Royal Navy. He welcomed his new responsibilities, delighted in the prominence the appointment as executive officer gave to him, and proceeded at once to justify the Admiralty's faith. From this point in his career the memoranda, recommendations, and reports began to flow from his pen; and, as he intended, their arrival at the desks of his captain, his commander-in-chief, and the various departments of the Admiralty served constantly to remind his seniors of his energy and his devotion to the service. They were not allowed for long to forget the existence of the commander of the *Warrior,* and later of the *Surprise* on the Mediterranean Station. While Albert Markham was writing his biographies of Sir John Franklin and John Davis and his books on the Far North, Tryon was submitting recommendations on the award of punishments, on the methods of dealing with leave-breaking and desertion, on docks accommodation and coaling facilities at various Spanish ports, on the provision of storage facilities at Gibraltar. When Tryon went ashore, perhaps at a small Greek port, he would examine the harbour and its approaches with a view to its use in the event of war, and his conclusions would within weeks be presented through his C.-in-C. to the Admiralty. In similar circumstances Albert Markham was more inclined to search out the nearest ruined temple and report its situation and condition to his cousin by letter. Except for occasional cricket, and shooting expeditions,[1] when Tryon invariably proved himself a crack shot, he gave all his time to his service, far beyond the range of his duties. He was becoming stout, from a natural physical indolence and from the hours he spent on paper work, and assuming the formidable and intimidating presence that was later to be so widely feared. Already he could be brusque and domineering, and quite incapable (in that quaint classical phrase so loved by Victorians and so frequently used of Tryon) of suffering fools gladly. By his early thirties he was fully aware of his destiny, expected, and too frequently received, the awed worship of his juniors. But he was scrupulously fair, cared a great deal for the welfare of the men, and was "endowed with a presence and manner and tact which tended to make him enthusiastically followed, while a strong will supporting a far-ranging ambition ensured respectful obedience."[2]

Honours, privileges, recognition, praise, and promotion —all come to George Tryon in such profusion that it seemed to his sometimes envious contemporaries as if he were outside the petty feuds and jealousies of the never-ending promotion struggle: a sort of Saturnian seaman, fated to prosper under every circumstance of service. "His

[1] In the Falkland Islands he and a party of four other officers once dispatched 409 wild geese, 26 snipe, 80 teal, 8 guanacos, 9 ducks, 4 oyster birds, and 24 dotterel.

[2] Colomb.

environment always suited him and he always suited his environment," wrote one of his fellow officers. "He had absolutely no difficulties to surmount." When he commanded the *Warrior,* the ship was ordered to escort Princess Alexandra of Denmark to London for her marriage to the Prince of Wales. The ship kept so close to the *Victoria and Albert,* "following her up through the intricate navigation of the estuary of the Thames, that the Princess Alexandra was greatly pleased at the performance of the monster ironclad, and requested that the signal might be made to the *Warrior* 'Princess is much pleased.' " In April 1866, after only five and a half years as a commander, he was promoted to post-captain—far ahead of his time, and far ahead of his contemporaries.

After his marriage in 1869—an eminently suitable and advantageous marriage to the Honourable Clementina Heathcote, daughter of Sir Gilbert Heathcote, Bart., created Baron Aveland—greater honours ashore and afloat followed. In April 1871 he was appointed as private secretary to the First Lord of the Admiralty, the Right Honourable G. J. Goschen, later Lord Goschen, the statesman and naval administrator. It was unprecedented for such a junior captain to be appointed to this responsible post—"a position in which a man of ability and of a strong personality can exercise great power for good or evil: more power in many cases than one of the Sea Lords of the Admiralty." And not for the first time there were complaints from those of greater seniority, who had watched his meteoric rise and themselves been passed over. Even in a service in which favouritism and nepotism had always been accepted, there was certain limits to the granting of favours. Now Tryon, already a holder of the Companionship of

Bath and an A.D.C. to Queen Victoria at the age of thirty-seven, had been encouraged to trespass beyond these limits, causing jealousy, according to his biographer, "amongst many of his less gifted seniors."

But once again George Tryon justified the trust shown in him, hurling himself into his new political life with gusto. In his two and a half years with Goschen he brought about many reforms, and was responsible for the establishment of greater social recognition of the Royal Navy, "in Court favours and honours, such as invitations to royal balls, concerts &c.," at parades and public festivities of all kinds. Understandably, this was a subject on which he felt strongly, and he could not have followed a better policy. Goschen was immensely gratified. The First Lord had, he reported at the end of Tryon's term of office, "an immensely high opinion not only of his naval knowledge, but of his general *savoir-faire*, rapidity of judgment, decision, extraordinary shrewdness, and great knowledge of men."

Ten years later Tryon was to return to the Admiralty, this time as Secretary, and he was the last serving officer to hold this immensely responsible post. But he was fully aware that to achieve the highest honours he must balance his career nicely between seagoing and shore administrative service. The command of the *Raleigh* in the crack Flying Squadron, and later of the *Monarch* in the Mediterranean Fleet, gave him full scope to demonstrate his seamanship—from the Falkland Islands to India, from the Dardanelles to the West Indies—and also on several occasions his skill and resourcefulness when it came to putting on a spectacle, always a highly regarded accomplishment in the Victorian Navy. On the royal visit of the Prince of Wales to Bombay there was great competition in the

accompanying squadron to put up the finest show at the
harbour illuminations; and no other captain could match
his bouquets of rockets and "his elaborate arrangements
for the simultaneous ignition of a hundred and two hundred
at a time." The *Raleigh* was especially favoured on that
occasion, and was ordered to escort the *Serapis* and the
royal yacht *Osborne* for the remainder of the Prince's
cruise, and on their journey back to England. This selection
was an honour, but it was also an embarrassment, for the
Raleigh was made custodian for many of the wild beasts
the Indian potentates had presented to the Prince of Wales,
none of which, out of courtesy, could be left behind. One
huge elephant refused even to board the train to Bombay,
but Tryon eventually sailed with two full-grown tigers,
Moody and Sankey; Jummoo, a full-grown leopard; and "a
large number of smaller and less formidable creatures,
including a good many birds"—all of which had to be
accommodated under the poop and tended by the crew.
Tryon, who was as punctilious about the cleanliness of his
ship as any naval commander, bore the ordeal stoically,
determined if possible to turn it to his advantage, and his
men did their best to feed and tend the beasts. Their
reward came when the Royal Squadron steamed through
the Solent, with half of England, or so it seemed, cheering
from the shores, an elephant standing on each of the
royal yacht's paddleboxes, and the *Raleigh*'s menagerie
howling in chorus with the welcoming salutes of the signal
guns.

Later that year the *Raleigh* was one of a number of
men-of-war of all nations which assembled at Smyrna to
see off her Royal and Imperial Highness the Duchess of
Edinburgh in the very fast Russian imperial yacht, the

Livadia. There were balls and receptions, "salutes and
illuminations, at which the *Raleigh* . . . made a good show,"
to precede her departure, but Tryon's real opportunity for
distinction came the next day, when the royal yacht
steamed down the Gulf of Smyrna at an ever-increasing
speed as if to challenge her numerous escorts. One after
another the other vessels were left behind, until the
Russian squadron itself was hull down astern, and at the
entrance to the gulf the *Raleigh* was the royal yacht's sole
escort. "The Duchess requested that a courteous signal
should be made to Captain Tryon thanking him for his
attendance and begging that he would not come any farther
out of his way: so Tryon prepared to 'part company'; but
before doing so he called upon his chief engineer to make
an effort and put on a spurt. The latter responded; up
rushed the *Raleigh* close alongside the *Livadia;* the ship's
company manned the rigging and gave three hearty cheers,
and the *Raleigh* sheered off and went on her way. Squibs,
crackers, and rockets were eclipsed; this was the real thing
—one of the leading factors of modern naval efficiency
demonstrated: Britain was justified of her stokers; and
Tryon was happy."[1] It was the sort of show at which
George Tryon excelled, with an admiring audience, and
in the presence of royalty and senior officials.

But if George Tryon was conscious of the importance
of "a good turn-out and a good show," he was also (with
Jackie Fisher, who served under him on the *Warrior* and
was one of his greatest admirers) the most down-to-earth
and realistic senior officer in the Royal Navy. By the 1880s
the Navy had not seen a fleet action for more than three
generations, and the service's experience of combat had

[1] Fitzgerald.

been limited to isolated minor actions, mainly against rebellious and ludicrously ill-equipped "natives." Even the competition between armour and guns that raged from the time of the launching of *La Gloire* and the *Warrior* was largely conjectural; and with the exhaustion of theoretical argument in every branch of the service there set in a period of stagnation in which the battleship came to be regarded less as a vessel intended for fighting in the line of battle and more as a ceremonial showpiece of glittering brass and paintwork and highly polished decks. The Manœuvring Book read like a glossary of ballet evolutions: elaborate, complex, spectacular, and prohibitive of all initiative. The signalling system was so bewilderingly ingenious that no one completely understood it, and to acquire a working knowledge took years of training. Steam engines were accepted only with the greatest reluctance, and for many years the engineers who operated them, and the coal they consumed—the disgusting mineral that tarnished brasswork, fouled decks and gangways, and smutted pure white canvas—were regarded with almost equal loathing. Whenever possible, the hated funnels were telescoped almost out of sight, propellers hoisted in, and boilers allowed to cool off. As a standard of excellence, seamanship reigned supreme; and it was considered vastly more creditable for a ship's crew to swarm aloft and spread every sail with speed and precision than to straddle a target at gunnery practice, even if the sails had long been rendered obsolete and the guns were in many cases primitive weapons compared with those of foreign navies.

George Tryon's ambition was no less than to bring about a revolution in the moribund principles that governed the Royal Navy towards the end of the nineteenth century. The accomplishment of this task required a man of enormous stature, but, as *The Times* once wrote, "in grasp of situation, rapidity of decision, and correctness of view, no naval commander of our day is, or has been, his superior. . . ." Only by confirming his reputation as a brilliant orthodox commander could he hope to overcome the counter-challenge of the conservative diehard elements in the Navy who had listened for so long to the comforting refrain of "Britannia Rules the Waves" that they had largely ceased to think of the service as a fighting force. But by 1887 Tryon was a rear admiral, a K.C.B., an officer of influence who had commanded in every corner of the Empire. He was the natural leader of a small group who were becoming aware of the Navy's dangerous weakness and stagnation —and their cause received an immense fillip from Tryon's evasion of the defending fleet and his subsequent "destruction" of Britain's ports in the 1888 manœuvres.

The most apparent result of the Achill Admiral's depredations was the 1889 Naval Defence Act, which made provision for the construction of seventy men-of-war in the next five years. It was not only the rebels who had been calling for greater naval expenditure for years past; there was no disagreement on this in the service. But Tryon knew that numerical parity with even three other combined powers was meaningless if the leadership was stultified and the crews were untrained for combat.

In the two years before his appointment to command the Mediterranean Fleet, Tryon opened two great campaigns: for the national insurance by the state of the country's merchant fleet in time of war, and for the drastic simplification of the system by which men-of-war manœuvred against an enemy and signalled to one another in action.

George Tryon failed in his lifetime in the cause of one campaign, and lost his life in the cause of the other.

Of his national-insurance scheme, Tryon wrote in the *United Service Magazine:* "In brief the proposal is . . . for the state to guarantee to pay the cost of vessels and cargoes destroyed by the enemy" to prevent the sudden rise of insurance premiums from driving every merchantman off the oceans on the outbreak of war. But this was so revolutionary a proposal that he could not hope for quick success. *The Times* thundered; London merchants claimed that it was an unnecessary and expensive measure. Arthur Forwood, the shipping tycoon, protested that "freedom from state interference in trade during war is even of more importance than in time of peace," and the P. & O.'s chairman considered that "the mere fact of the government paying for the ships captured would not diminish famine prices to any sensible extent." It was to be a long campaign and one which continued after Tryon's death and achieved success only a few weeks before the outbreak of the First World War.

One naval correspondent aboard Tryon's flagship at Berehaven in 1888 had reported, "There is no branch of the naval service more important, no department from the failure of which greater calamity might result in the hour of need, than that of the signals, and yet in the *Hercules* there are only five men who can take in signals." Tryon was perfectly aware of this deficiency; it had been a matter of great concern to him for years. The elementary procedure of passing messages rapidly between ships at sea had been elaborated over the years of peace into a highly complex system of flags of different patterns, different shapes and colours, the meaning of which could be changed by hoisting one flag or group of flags superior to another, or by hoisting a ball above or below. A ship could hoist a number of signals on different masts and yards, which then had to be read, sometimes at a great distance through a glass in misty weather, by taking them in a prescribed order.

Fourteen thousand variations of signals were considered the minimum requirement of a fleet in daytime; and even Colomb[1] considered that "our naval night signals are now more inefficient than they were in the middle of the last century." The signal books were huge volumes containing voluminous instructions for every conceivable description of formation and manœuvre, most of which required long hoists of many coloured flags; and the ships' captains—and the fleet's C.-in-C.—were so obstructed by the signalmen bustling about with their bunting and halyards on the confined space of the bridge that it was even sometimes difficult to see what the other ships of the squadron were doing. Signalling, George Tryon considered, had become a cult—a thoroughly dangerous cult. In action, even presuming that the smoke of battle had not obscured the admiral's signals and the captains' replies, the first burst of accurate enemy fire would mow down the exposed signallers and tear to shreds their elaborate strings of coloured flags. It was some measure of the Admiralty's condition of peaceful torpor that it was necessary for George Tryon to point this out to them.

When, on September 21, 1891, Vice-Admiral Sir George Tryon assumed command of Her Majesty's Ships and Vessels on the Mediterranean Station, he was at last given the opportunity he had been waiting for to put his theories into practice. Soon after his arrival he issued a memorandum to

[1] *Journal of the Royal United Services Institute.*

all ships captains. "I have long been impressed," he wrote, "with the importance of exercising a fleet from the point where the drill books leave off. . . . It is apparent to me that a fleet that can be rapidly manœuvred without having to wait for a series of signal repetitions and replies will be at a great advantage. . . ." His subordinates awaited the inevitable next step with some anxiety. They had only a short time to wait, and the result was even more revolutionary and simple—even frighteningly simple—than they could have anticipated. In future, the Mediterranean Fleet was to play follow my leader.

George Tryon's plan was called "The T.A. System, a system of fleet manœuvres with and without signals." Under its operation the signaller would be virtually eliminated. "The design and object of the T.A. System," wrote Tryon, "is to provide for the time when no signals are reasonably to be relied upon." Under it "absolute precision is not to be expected in manœuvres, but a very little practice will show that sufficient accuracy for safety and all practical purposes is easily secured." All that was necessary to put the system into effect was for the flagship to raise the two code flags "TA"; from that moment, the ships of the squadron, whether in single line ahead, two divisions line ahead of four subdivisions line ahead, merely observed the movements of the flagship or the guides of the divisions, following the turns like children in a playground at follow my leader. Tryon's belief—later borne out in practice—was that almost every evolution a fleet might require in action could be carried out simply by observation of the flagship's own movements. But if greater precision was at any time required, orthodox signals could still be made, and Tryon constantly stressed that T.A. was a supplementary, not a substitute, form of signalling; that it might, or might not, apply at any time during manœuvres, even days after the initial "TA" had been hoisted. Ships on manœuvres, he frequently told his subordinates, "are constantly under the influence of 'TA.' " Perhaps the most important benefit of this form of signalling, from Tryon's point of view, was that it emphasized freedom of initiative, the wide choice of action permitted both to a C.-in-C. and to all his captains.

If only because it made a mockery of the eleborate system of manœuvring signals that had been practised for decades, TA was hardly likely to be given a warm welcome. Retired admirals were outraged, serving admirals hostile or suspicious. There was hardly a flag officer in the service who welcomed the innovation. "Unsound in theory and perilous in practice," *The Times* called it.

The naval careers of Albert Markham and George Tryon had touched and crossed briefly, and only once, in the past thirty-five years, when, during those blockade days off Berehaven, they had faced each other as protagonists: the tense and nervous jailer and the wily imprisoned Achill Admiral. Three years later Tryon had no say in the choice of his second-in-command, and when it was made he had no particular cause for alarm. From all he had heard, Markham would make an adequate Number Two. He certainly had no wish for a strong personality; he asked of him only loyalty, reasonable intelligence, a willingness to accept unorthodoxy, and a sufficient sense of responsibility to control, under his orders, the activities of the second division, which for most of the year cruised independently in the Levant.

The two men met for the first time as C.-in-C. and

second-in-command in March of 1892. Markham was then just fifty years old, Tryon sixty. Superficially there was a certain similarity between the two men. Both had keen brown eyes and weather-beaten skin above their full beards, were inclined to baldness and stoutness, and were tall and straight-backed. But everything about Tryon suggested greater positivity and purpose; there was no trace of hesitancy in his speech and movements, and his advantage of inches in girth and stature over Markham, the strength in his shoulders and his bull neck, all confirmed the immense authority of the decision-maker. As naval officers, the contrast between the two admirals was striking and obvious to the humblest ordinary seaman: the one, wholly dedicated to his service, domineering, irascible, utterly self-confident; the other the loyal and earnest amateur, tetchy with his subordinates in his anxiety to please his superiors. There could be no question who was the more valuable officer to the service, nor who deserved from his country the higher honours. As men, the contrast was equally strong, but their qualities and faults, which were less easy to define and more difficult to place in balance, were to be put to the test and exposed to the world in the tragedy that lay ahead.

4

ON GOOD FRIDAY, APRIL 13, 1893, the flagship of the
Mediterranean Fleet was recommissioned at Malta. Thirteen wardroom officers were turned over to the new commission.

Vice-Admiral Sir George Tryon's flagship, H.M.S.
Victoria, had been nicknamed "the slipper" since she was
first commissioned three years before. It was difficult to
take the *Victoria* seriously, even in that period of bizarre
naval architecture. There were perhaps only one or two
worse battleships serving in the navies of the world, but
her launching in the Queen's Golden Jubilee year had been
accompanied by a stream of stunning statistics and extravagant praise, and Her Majesty was presented with a magnificent silver scale model of the vessel by the officers of the
Royal Navy and the Royal Marines. The ship was, it was
said, the most powerful ironclad afloat—the fastest; and one
of the largest; the most strongly protected, with a solid foot-
and-a-half wall of compound steel amidships; the most
heavily armed, with massive 16.25-inch guns. With such
extreme and apparently formidable features, she seemed
the perfect flagship for the proud Mediterranean Fleet and
its heroic and popular commander-in-chief. Next to an

admiral, the British people dearly loved a great battleship.

She was called "the slipper"—or, with her later sister ship, "the pair of slippers"—for her long, low forecastle, which seemed to disappear entirely in any sort of sea, leaving her battery deck and upper works, her fore-and-aft bridge, and her tall twin side-by-side funnels wallowing on the ocean in frightening detachment. On this forward deck, a bare fifteen feet above the sea, were placed, in a vast single turret, the ship's main armament, the twin guns, the calibre, weight, shell, range, and penetrating power of which were quoted with such pride by contemporary naval correspondents. They were mounted as low as this to avoid too great instability, and placed forward in this unusual way, it was understood at the time, for the special purpose of forcing a passage through the Dardanelles in the event of a second war in the Black Sea, there having been yet another Russian scare in the year she was laid down. These guns were 111-ton weapons, the largest in the Royal Navy, the largest in the world, clumsy to train, slow to fire, thoroughly unreliable and—to their crews as well as to any potential enemy—the most feared guns in the fleet. The Armstrong 111-ton gun was the final folly of three decades of ordinance mismanagement, when, in a frenzy of vacillation, muzzle-loaders had given way to breech-loaders, which were replaced again by muzzle-loaders, until one of H.M.S. *Thunderer*'s 12.5-inch weapons blew up, killing most of the men in the turret.[1] The *Victoria*'s main breech-loading armament was at least as dangerous, and the guns' barrels were so long and so heavy that when they were first fitted

---

[1] Tryon was present on this occasion, on another battleship, and, after dispatching doctors to assist the wounded, returned to the target "and blazed away with the heaviest charge to show that the guns were not going to burst."

the muzzles drooped. Sir William Armstrong blandly explained this away by saying that the carriage did not support them properly and they had naturally sagged of their own weight. The remedy was quite simple: the gunners would simply have to give the weapon a little more elevation "and the projectile would arrive at its destination just the same." The *Victoria*'s guns were rarely fired, for fear of damage to the ship's structure. The blast and recoil effects were dreaded by officers and men alike. When they were fired forward, they buckled the deck; when fired abaft the beam, the blast played havoc with the bridgework. "These monsters are treated with a sort of gingerly consideration, which leaves the impression that they are privately regarded as a highly respectable blunder," Lord George Hamilton once referred to them. But publicly, and by foreign naval powers, they were regarded with mixed wonder and awe. Even if the *Victoria* did "draw too much water to cross Sandy Hook bar," as the New York *Tribune*'s naval correspondent pointed out, "she could come near enough to send death-dealing projectiles into the Fifth Avenue Hotel." But it is doubtful if the poor *Victoria*'s clumsy monstrosities could have carried out their intended function and even hit the towering cliffs as she steamed up the Dardanelles.

The *Victoria* was a brand-new ship, only three months old, when George Tryon assumed command of the Mediterranean Fleet. With her sister ship, the *Sans Pareil,* and some ten more ironclads and supporting cruisers and light craft—a force superior on paper to that of any other nation's entire navy—he proceeded at once to put into practice his revolutionary theories of fleet management. The reaction of his subordinates to their new C.-in-C.'s casual attitude to everything relating to signalling and squadron evolutions, which they had always held to be sacred, varied from grave suspicion to enthusiasm. Such men as Arthur Wilson and Reginald Custance considered the T.A. System dangerously unorthodox, while the second division's senior captain, Gerard Noel, recognized at once the value of any system of communication which would reduce the number of signals "clogging the signal book with hundreds of words that have no material bearing on naval subjects."

No doubt some of the criticism of T.A. by his captains reached Tryon's ears, but never directly. He was by now the most formidable figure in the Royal Navy, with an equal capacity for instilling fear, loyalty, and confidence in those serving under him. Because one of his chief ambitions was to break up the traditionalism that had paralysed initiative in the Navy for half a century, he would often deliberately express outrageous theories or order unconventional evolutions; anything would do to shock his subordinates into a state of alertness. "He realized the importance of the personality of a commander in high command," wrote an officer[1] serving under him at the time, "and perhaps posed a little, not by any means from smallness of nature, but for the good of the Service, and he would not have objected to the Tryon Touch inspiring in his captains the same confidence that the Nelson Touch did in those of old days. He was a very big man, with a dominating personality, and he had a way which has been described as making his two eyes look like one, which seemed to bore through you."

For a time even George Tryon was unable to convince some of the captains of the Mediterranean Fleet that the system of signals on which they had been brought up, and

[1] *Memories of a Marine,* by Major-General Sir George Aston (1919).

which had been practised for decades, was other than the
best. But they could not forever entirely resist his enthusiasm, and partly by intimidation, partly by instilling in
them some of his own abundant self-confidence, he had the
whole fleet carrying out the free-and-easy follow-my-leader
T.A. System of evolutions during the combined late summer manœuvres of 1892 with some show of confidence, although numerous mistakes were made.

At the end of a period of exercises, Tryon would sum-
mon all captains to the flagship, and, when they had
assembled in his large, elaborately and comfortably fur-
nished cabin in the stern of the *Victoria,* would produce
from a drawer in his mahogany desk a collection of model
battleships, which he would lay out in formation on the top
of the circular table in the centre of the cabin, accompanying his explanations with rapidly drawn diagrams on sheets
of paper and with sharp questions, reprimands, and advice.
Tryon would simulate the evolutions they had just carried
out, movement by movement, leaning his great bulk across
the table in order to shift the positions of the models in
turn, striving to stir up controversy, and even making assertions that were patently false in order to set off an argument.
The first thing he demanded of his captains was enthusiasm.
Without enthusiasm, he knew, he could get nowhere with
them. Some responded strongly to this encouragement,
others held back, nervous of the bellow that might greet
their assertions; for, as one officer[1] recalled, "all who knew
him were aware of the undefined limits which enclosed
these discussions, and some never got up to them." At other
times, as the fleet steamed back towards Malta, he might
make a signal that he would meet his captains at his office

[1] Colomb.

on the Strada Mezzedi in Valetta, or on the Corradino, the huge naval parade ground, where, Goodenough remembered,[1] "he would draw from their ideas, pouncing on those without any, and 'breaking a lance' with those who did. He was big," this same officer described him at this time, "big in figure, big in ideas, his generosity equal to his ideas, massive, constructive, and a man of the world and of a big world. There was something in him that inspired his subordinates with confidence in every order and direction that he gave."

Tryon spent a great deal of his time, and much more than he would have preferred, at his office desk in Malta on administrative work; and his duties as C.-in-C. included the usual formal reviews and receptions of royalty and distinguished visitors at foreign ports and at his home base. In the spring of 1893 he and Lady Tryon had to receive and entertain the newly married Prince and Princess Ferdinand of Bulgaria, to attend Queen Victoria during her visit to Florence, escort the Princess of Wales and her two daughters on a tour of the island, and, in April, welcome the First and Second Lords of the Admiralty, with the First Lord's wife, Lady Spencer. The Sea Lords were shown over the dockyard and the naval buildings and inspected the men of the fleet on the Corradino at battalion and physical drill under arms—two thousand of them in white flannel shirts and blue trousers "swinging their rifles as one man to the sound of the music of the massed bands of the fleet."[2] Lord Spencer was apparently satisfied with the C.-in-C. and pleased by all he saw, for two months later, in the Upper House, he reported of Tryon: "I lately had an opportunity of seeing

[1] *A Rough Record,* by Admiral Sir William Goodenough (1943).
[2] *Memories of a Bluejacket,* by Patrick Riley (1927).

him at his post and I think I may say that he not only had
the fullest and highest confidence of my colleagues at the
Admiralty and myself, but he also had the fullest confidence
of every officer and man who served under him, and who
were proud to have him as their leader."

It had been a trying spring: first there was this particularly heavy round of social engagements; then there had
been an unusually persistent outbreak of that bane of
Mediterranean service, Malta fever;[1] and Tryon was suffering from a nasty ulcer on his leg, perhaps caused by worry
and pressure of work, for as a rule, and considering his
weight, he kept very healthy. He was thankful that the
end of May was in sight, and that soon the fleet would be
at sea again for the summer manœuvres.

At last, on May 27, the first division, with the second
division's flagship, H.M.S. *Camperdown,* weighed and proceeded out of Malta harbour in single line: six of the world's
most powerful battleships, their white upper works and
brass glinting in the brilliant afternoon sun, their shallow
bows already dipping into the moderate seas beyond the
breakwaters, black smoke from a dozen tall funnels drifting
high astern, blending together, and dissolving into the blue
above. From the roof of the chart house, forward on the
Victoria, Tryon watched the squadron forming up as the
white buildings of Valetta and the coastline of the island
faded in the heat haze. From the leather-padded chair always
provided for him on the deck over the chart house, Tryon
could see four hundred yards astern the brass stem-piece of
the *Camperdown,* the broad black-painted hull, the froth

---

[1] Sir Robert Ross eventually traced this to the island's goats, and
when their milk was banned to the fleet the fever ceased.

of the bow wave rising and falling with her pitch, and the projecting steel ram slicing through the water. It was six months since he had been to sea with Markham; he was hoping for a performance more up to "Mediterranean form" from his second-in-command this year.

Course was North 84 East 48'. Down on the mess deck, the men off watch were finishing supper. In two hours it would be dark.

Albert Markham's first thirteen months as Rear Admiral to Tryon had been a period of almost continuous anxiety, broken only by visits to the richer historical sites of the Levant, and several weeks of recuperating from a sharp dose of Malta fever.

On his appointment as second-in-command in March 1892, he proceeded to Malta, where he met Tryon and was briefed about the T.A. System, the forthcoming summer manœuvres, and the second division's role in the Levant and in Egyptian waters, where it was normally stationed, and where it frequently became involved as a weapon of influence and pressure. Markham then left for Alexandria, where he at once found himself involved in a complicated political situation. The Turks were at that time busily attempting to appropriate from Egypt the Sinai Peninsula, which would have given them virtual control of the north end of the Suez Canal; and Sir Evelyn Baring, with the support of Kitchener's Egyptian Army, was concerned to prevent this, without, if possible, giving offence to anyone or creating any sort of fracas. It was not a critical situation, but it was one that required the squadron's presence a great deal longer than Tryon thought advisable, and Markham found himself torn between the wishes of his

C.-in-C. that he leave and take his squadron on exercises, and those of the persuasive Baring, who wanted him to remain.

As soon as he could get away from Alexandria, Markham began to try out for the first time the T.A. system so that he could show some familiarity with it when his squadron met Tryon's first division for the combined manœuvres. He found it difficult to operate at first, and felt lost and, in certain circumstances, helpless without the support that the familiar series of elaborate fluttering signals normally gave a commander. He recorded at the time that he thought the system "required much practice," and he also doubted whether it would work in action, the eventuality for which Tryon had, of course, especially intended it.

But between exercises, courses, gunnery trials, and torpedo practice, Markham was able to spend a certain amount of time ashore, indulging the one interest that he had kept all through his service career. At Mycenae he saw "the Treasure House of Atreus and the other beehive tombs"; at Rhodes "it would be impossible to describe all we saw"; on the coast of Thessaly he made an expedition to the monasteries of Meteora. Corinth, Eleusis, and Samos were all visited; and the details of every expedition to every shrine and tomb and crumbling ruin were recorded as meticulously as ever in the journal he still carried with him. The high point of the summer cruise was reached when he managed to arrange a rendezvous with Clements and tour with him the old fortress of The Knights of St. John ("still in a wonderful state of preservation") when the squadron was anchored off Budrum.

Soon after this he received orders to join up with Tryon

for the joint exercises; and for three anxious weeks the
delights of archaeology and historical exploration had to be
put aside as he struggled with a still unfamiliar system of
signalling and manœuvring and endeavoured to reach the
standard of perfection set by a demanding and irritable
C.-in-C. Markham did his best, as he had always done his
best in every command he had held; but he could never
hope to match the performance set by Tryon, who made
no allowance for the fact that his second-in-command was
new to the station and to his own unusual methods. Time
after time when Markham was slow to respond or showed
a lack of precision or initiative, a public signal of reprimand
would be made on the *Victoria*.

It was a relief when the squadrons completed their combined manœuvres and reached Malta in the middle of
November; and Markham was happier still when he received orders early in January to sail east with the ships
of his division. He left on the seventh, "glad to be afloat
again." But within a few weeks he was struck down by a
particularly fierce attack of Malta fever, followed by acute
rheumatism, which left him weak and useless for seagoing
service. He took a leisurely convalescence at Fiume and
Athens. By early April, Tryon was impatient to complete
preparations for the summer cruise, and ordered Markham
back to Malta to take command of his temporary flagship,
the *Camperdown,* and sail her to rejoin the second division,
then cruising off the coasts of Greece and Turkey under
the senior captain, Noel. But Markham was still not satisfied with the state of his health and informed Tryon that
he would be delayed several more weeks. Clements and
Minna had arrived in Sicily, and Markham could not resist
the chance of seeing them together again before leaving

for the Levant with his C.-in-C. He spent several happy weeks at Taormina with them, and "after a fortnight considered himself fit for the ascent of Monte Venere, which he thoroughly enjoyed."[1]

Markham arrived at Malta at last on May 24, Queen Victoria's birthday, which was acknowledged with the royal salute of twenty-one guns from the ships in the harbour; and in the early afternoon he visited his temporary flagship for three-quarters of an hour before leaving for the home of the dockyard superintendent, Vice-Admiral Richard Tracey, where he had been invited to stay. Three days later the *Camperdown*, flying the flag of Rear Admiral Markham, proceeded out of Malta harbour two cables astern of the *Victoria*.

George Tryon had worked out a full and elaborate programme for the joint manœuvres of the Mediterranean Fleet that summer. Several of the dozen ironclads under his command, particularly those of the second division, which had not exercised so frequently with him, were unsatisfactory. In the course of the next six weeks Tryon was determined to sharpen up their captains and crews, to instill into them some enterprise and some of the confidence they still lacked in the loose, free-moving T.A. system of evolutions. He was going to surprise them with sudden and unusual orders, alter the formation of his men-of-war with daring unorthodoxy, carry out exercises at night, on all occasions matching the conditions and circumstances as closely as possible to those that would apply in a real war. Above all, he hoped to create more confidence and a

[1] *The Life of Sir Albert Hastings Markham,* by M. E. and F. A. Markham (1927).

greater sense of drive and willingness in his second-in-command; for at no time during his fourteen months' service in the Mediterranean could Tryon pretend that Albert Markham had been a satisfactory rear admiral. He seemed to lack the ability to concentrate, to make quick decisions, and to anticipate situations in the rapidly changing circumstances of fleet evolutions. Tryon found him an exasperating pupil.

There were evolutions during the second afternoon at sea, and right through until after midnight; there were gunnery drill and target practice with the battleships' secondary armament, and torpedo practice. After they joined up with the second division at sea off Marmarica, and Markham had taken over from Captain Noel, more elaborate manœuvres with the increased number of ironclads could be attempted. From Marmarica, where they coaled and rested for a few days, the combined fleet proceeded to Acre, and then to Haifa—a town which disappointed Markham and which he found barren, "a long, sandy coast, with Carmel rising in the background, and a few olive trees, dates, figs, etc., growing at its foot."

Their stay at Haifa was brief, allowing Markham only a quick visit to the Convent of Elias on Mount Carmel. On June 16 they proceeded to sea again for Beirut, carrying out more exercises on the way. . . .

5

I'm paying a hurried visit to the coast of Syria; it does us all a lot of good being together.

Admiral Tryon, in a letter to the Director of Naval Intelligence, dated 16 June, 1893

AT A QUARTER TO TEN on the morning of June 22, 1893, the combined Mediterranean Fleet weighed anchor at Beirut and proceeded to sea. It had been a pleasant five days at the Syrian port. There had been leave for everyone and the weather had remained clear and warm, and if the delights ashore were restricted for the bluejackets to doubtful food, drink, and women, they expected nothing more from an eastern Mediterranean sea town. Some of the officers had hired underfed and scruffy-looking ponies and explored the hinterland for something to shoot at. Admiral Markham found time for two excursions on horseback to Baalbec and Damascus, visiting ancient ruins and tombs and temples. Admiral Tryon, on the other hand, was confined to his cabin for most of the time, working at his papers and planning to the last detail the programme of the fleet for the rest of the manœuvres. His entertainment was limited to one brief but successful shooting trip, which he made against the advice of his doctor, Fleet Surgeon Herbert McKay Ellis, who had been treating the small ulcer that still would not heal. The only event of importance during the sojourn had been the ceremony of June 20, when, at 8 a.m., all ships had been dressed in honour of the anniversary of Queen Victoria's accession to the throne; and at noon the harbour had echoed to the combined royal salute of twenty-one guns from every battleship.

The departure from Beirut, like almost all fleet departures from port or anchorage under Tryon, was unorthodox, and no other C.-in-C. in the Royal Navy was likely even to have attempted it. They had been anchored in two columns parallel to the shore, the first division, headed by the *Victoria,* nearer the land. But instead of proceeding in that order in line abreast to sea, as soon as they were aweigh Tryon ordered the first division between the ships of the second division and at a higher speed, then slowed and signalled to Markham to catch him up on a diagonal course until the whole fleet was brought together exactly in single line abreast. It was the sort of daring evolution that Tryon relished, the sort of evolution he had already sprung on the fleet several times over the past weeks.

By 10 o'clock the fleet was clear of the anchorage and in the open sea, and at 10:30 course was altered to north by east, still in single line abreast, and the speed set at 8.2 knots. Tripoli, the fleet's next port of call, lay rather less than sixty miles up the Syrian coast, and they expected to be anchored again by 4:30 p.m. It appeared likely to be an uneventful trip as there was little time for more surprise evolutions if they were to anchor before dark. However, with Tryon everyone had to be prepared for the unexpected, and a strict lookout was kept for signals from the *Victoria.*

In the morning Fleet Surgeon Ellis went down to Tryon's cabin at the stern of the flagship and examined the admiral's leg. He was pleased to find that the ulcer was at last responding to treatment. "I am very glad to say, sir, that in a couple of days I shall be able to wipe my hands of you, and I am

sure you'll be glad," he told him. Ellis enjoyed these visits
and would miss them. They usually talked together on
some general subject for a time, which both officers found
relaxing. "I could not help on these occasions admiring the
great versatility of his mind, and the accuracy and range
of his general information," Ellis recounted later.

Surgeon Ellis had already called in at the ship's sick bay,
and he had followed this with a visit to Midshipman Harold
W. Gambier, who was so poorly that he had been given
Tryon's spare cabin. His last call was on the ship's com-
mander, John R. Jellicoe, later Admiral of the Fleet Lord
Jellicoe, C.-in-C. of the Grand Fleet in World War I and
Britain's most famous naval figure of the twentieth century.
Both the officers were suffering from Malta fever and had
high temperatures. There was little Ellis could do beyond
giving them doses of quinine.

The eleven ironclads[1] and two light cruisers were spread
out in a line two miles wide, each pushing up an identical
bow wave, each followed by its attendant sea birds, the
black smoke from their funnels forming into a huge cloud
that fell only slowly astern in the still air. Ten miles away,
across an almost flat calm sea, the coastline of Syria appeared as a faint olive line, the mountains of Lebanon
floating in a detached world of their own above it. From
time to time flags fluttered at the yardarm of the *Victoria*
or the *Camperdown,* ordering one or another of the ships
to adjust her position, and speed was at once checked or
increased in obedience. To its six thousand men the
ritualistic grandeur of the Mediterranean Fleet at sea was
accepted as a commonplace; but it was a sight that had
succeeded for generations in impressing the countries of

[1] Eight battleships and three first-class armoured cruisers.

the Levant with Britain's strength. Sheikhs and potentates, kings and sultans, had fallen or been raised by its power, which had frustrated the ambitions of Russia, gently curbed Turkish expansionism, and influenced time and again the policies of France and Italy, the Balkan countries, and, in some degree, every state in Europe and the Near East.

At 12:40 the *Victoria* hoisted a signal giving instructions for anchoring at Tripoli. One after another the acknowledgements came in from the ships of the two divisions; and forty minutes later speed was increased to 8.8 knots and course altered to northeast by north. "TA" had not been rescinded since it had first been hoisted some days before, but these instructions were, of course, transmitted in the orthodox manner. Sixteen miles ahead the Tower of the Lions, the ancient fortress standing above Tripoli, was just visible from the crow's-nest. In little more than two hours the fleet would be at rest again. Dinner of salt pork and pea soup had been served on the mess decks of the battleships and had been supplemented by the canteen, where more appetizing food was served at low rates— chocolate, some fruit, and a cup of hot, sweet tea. It was Thursday, "make-and-mend" afternoon, "a time sacred in the routine of every well-regulated ship to the bluejackets' holiday—a holiday which is, by law, supposed to be devoted to the making and mending of his clothes," wrote a contemporary naval correspondent, "but which he more often devotes to smoking, chatter and slumber. We can fancy that on that sultry afternoon, with the hot sun overhead throwing a glare across the almost calm sea, the inclination to work was not great."

In the gunroom the midshipmen off watch retired to their hammocks after some mild horseplay; and in the wardrooms those officers not sipping coffee or chattering quietly were sprawled out in the leather armchairs, asleep. By two o'clock more than half the officers and men of the Mediterranean Fleet were either sound asleep or dozing below decks in the humid air.

On board the flagship, Vice-Admiral Sir George Tryon left his sternwalk, where he had been taking a stroll after his luncheon, and retired to his adjoining cabin. He was, as usual, little affected by the warm, damp air, but was conscious of the deplorably lethargic atmosphere that over-hung his fleet. A straightforward passage from one anchor-age to another in the middle of summer manœuvres was not to be countenanced. Officers and men needed waking up after the five slack days at Beirut; and there is little doubt that Tryon made the decision at this time to set a real challenge to his ships' captains, and in particular to Rear Admiral Markham. If they were to make this dull passage between the two Syrian ports, at least he would see to it that the fleet's entry into Tripoli would be no less interest-ing than its departure from Beirut. He would set them one final evolution that would tax the skill of even such ex-perienced captains as Noel of the *Nile* and Wilson of the *Victoria*'s sister ship, the *Sans Pareil*.

Tryon rang the bell for an orderly to fetch his flag captain, Maurice Bourke, and the *Victoria*'s staff com-mander, Thomas Hawkins-Smith, and sat down at his desk to await their arrival.

Hawkins-Smith was a grizzled officer of the old school who had been brought up under sail and, like so many of his contemporaries, felt that the Royal Navy would never be the same since its abandonment. He was admirably conscientious, and one could call him an able officer with-

out sounding uncharitable. The Honourable Maurice
Bourke, his junior in years if senior in rank, on the other
hand, had readily accepted the new order, which had been
established while he was still a midshipman, and had
jumped his promotion with something of the ease and
facility that his commander-in-chief had shown. He was
clean-shaven, dashing in appearance, and exceptionally
handsome, "as attractive as any other Bourke," Goodenough wrote in his memoirs, "and that's saying a good
deal." Bourke had even survived the grounding of the
Victoria[1] for six days near Plataea, on the coast of Greece,
and the subsequent court martial a year before. Flag Captain Bourke had as promising a future as any officer in the
fleet.

The two officers entered the commander-in-chief's cabin,
Hawkins-Smith with the appropriate charts under his arm.

"What's our position now?" Tryon asked Hawkins-Smith.

The staff commander spread one of the charts on the
table in the centre of the cabin and pointed it out. "I
suggest we alter course to east by north, sir."

"At what distance from Rankine lighthouse will that
take us?"

Rankine lighthouse was on one of the last of the rocky
islands that stretched out to sea from the Tower of the
Lions and the town of Tripoli and formed the eastern side
of Tripoli Bay. (See map on page 129.)

"Exactly two and a half miles, sir."

"And how far will that take us off the anchorage?"

Hawkins-Smith assured the admiral that the distance

---

[1] This had occurred during torpedo trials when the ship was only
a few months old, and had caused considerable concern in England.
Tryon was not on board at the time, but arrived on the scene shortly
afterwards to supervise the elaborate arrangements for her refloating.

would be over three and a half miles, and Tryon looked down again at the chart. "That will do very well," he said, "as it will give the ships time to get into their stations before anchoring." He then described with a pointer the evolution he had in mind to bring the fleet into its anchorage. "I shall form the fleet into columns of two divisions, six cables apart, and reverse the course by turning inwards. You look out for the times, Hawkins-Smith."

It at once occurred to the staff commander that a distance of six cables (or twelve hundred yards) between the two divisions, if they were to turn inwards, was dangerously close; but even to make a comment on such an elementary point to the commander-in-chief required some courage, especially as evolutions were not within his province. Perhaps he had misunderstood the instruction. But before leaving, Hawkins-Smith remarked tentatively, "It will require at least eight cables for that, sir."

Abstractedly, and after a moment's hesitation, Tryon replied, "Yes, it shall be eight cables."

Partly reassured, Hawkins-Smith left at once for the forebridge with the charts, and Tryon rang for his flag lieutenant, Richard Charles, Lord Gillford, the son of the Right Honourable Admiral Richard James, the Earl of Clanwilliam, K.C.B., K.C.M.G., C.-in-C., Portsmouth. Gillford had been Tryon's flag lieutenant since the latter had assumed command of the Mediterranean Station in 1891 and was more familiar with the methods, the strength, and the eccentricities of the commander-in-chief than anyone else in the fleet. Tryon had no close confidant among his staff and never discussed his plans even with Lord Gillford, but after acting as his flag lieutenant on two series of major summer manœuvres and on innumerable voyages up and down the Mediterranean, the younger man was by now able to divine when his commander-in-chief was plotting some particularly surprising evolution. Clearly this was such an occasion.

When the flag lieutenant entered the cabin, Tryon was sitting in a seat on the port side of his sternwalk. Lord Gillford passed by Captain Bourke, who was standing between the admiral and the cabin door, and saluted.

"Will you make a signal to form columns of divisions line ahead, columns disposed abeam to port," Tryon told him. "And make the columns six cables apart." To emphasize this point, he passed him a piece of paper on which was scribbled the figure 6. Bourke was too far away to see what Tryon had written, and Lord Gillford did not comment on the fact that there was nothing else on the paper, although later he said, "I should have expected that he would have written 'Columns to be six' or something like that."

Lord Gillford left and climbed up to the after bridge, where he gave the order to the yeoman to bend on the signal. By 2:10 the flags were fluttering at the yardarm, and were acknowledged in turn by the *Camperdown* and the rest of the fleet. A moment later Hawkins-Smith came hurrying aft.

"Haven't you made a mistake?" the staff commander asked the flag lieutenant in some agitation, "as the admiral said the columns were to be eight cables."

"No, I think not," Lord Gillford replied, and produced the slip of paper with the figure 6 on it.

Hawkins-Smith glanced down at it but was still not satisfied. "I am sure the admiral intended it to be eight. Will you please go down to his cabin again to make certain?"

It was an uncomfortable sort of mission, but Lord Gill-ford did as he was told, and found Captain Bourke still with Tryon in his cabin. "The staff commander asked me to remind you that you had agreed to eight cables, sir," he said.

"You certainly said it was to be more than six cables, sir," Bourke added anxiously.

Tryon looked up from his desk. He was not pleased. "Leave it at six cables," he said brusquely. It was a long time since two of his officers had questioned an order.

"Yes, sir," Lord Gillford left at once, returned to the after bridge, and sent a message by one of the signallers to confirm to Hawkins-Smith that the commander-in-chief was adamant.

With the lowering of the signal from the flagship just after 2:20, all the vessels with the exception of the two flagships reduced speed and ported their helms in order to slip, in two divisions, behind the *Victoria* and *Camperdown*, which then closed to within six cables of each other. It was a simple evolution, which the fleet had carried out many times. H.M.S. *Edinburgh* of the second division fell out of station by a few degrees, and was told by the *Camperdown* that it would have been better if she had kept her flagship on a compass bearing; and the *Amphion* fell behind a shade and was told to increase speed. By 2:35, with the anchorage at Tripoli now only eight miles distant, the evolution had been successfully completed, and ten minutes later course was altered to east by north, the first division decreasing, and the second division increasing, speed to preserve station.

Captain Bourke came up onto the forebridge at about this time. He was as concerned as the staff commander and the flag lieutenant had been at the proposed evolution, and when he met Hawkins-Smith on deck again told him helplessly, "He won't go to more than six cables."

By now the captain of every ship was on his bridge in preparation for anchoring, curious to discover the method Tryon would employ to get his nine ironclads and two accompanying light cruisers into Tripoli roads on their correct anchorage bearings. It was already evident that, as so often occurred, the approach would be an unorthodox one. The comment later of the *Edinburgh*'s captain, John William Brackenbury, was typical of the fleet's attitude towards their admiral. "You know how accustomed we were to brilliant manœuvres, which afterwards the C.-in-C. would explain, and generally show the exact calculations he had made." Only on the *Victoria* was there any real anxiety, and even on the flagship no one but Captain Bourke, Staff Commander Hawkins-Smith, and Flag Lieutenant Lord Gillford, the three officers who were aware of Tryon's apparently dangerous intentions, were at all concerned.

Half an hour later Tryon emerged from his cabin, made his way up onto deck and then more slowly, pausing once or twice to regain his breath, up the ladder to the after-bridge. He placed his hands on the rail forward and glanced to port to the *Camperdown* a little less than three-quarters of a mile away, and the four ships of Markham's second division in line ahead behind her, separated from one another by a distance of only four hundred yards.

Astern of the *Victoria* he saw the *Nile, Dreadnought, Inflexible, Collingwood,* and *Phaeton.* The nearest battleship was the *Nile,* her two tall funnels in tandem, her twin 13.5-inch 67-ton guns pointing forward in their turret—

the newest, the heaviest, and most heavily armoured battleship in the fleet, with a belt of compound steel amidships
no less than twenty inches thick. If anyone should make an
error in the forthcoming evolution Tryon had planned, it
would not be Gerard Henry Uctred Noel, the *Nile*'s captain, the officer Tryon would prefer to any other as second-
in-command in the event of a fleet action against an enemy.
On the landward side of the *Victoria* the Rankine lighthouse stood up clearly only two and a half miles away, and
beyond could be seen the white buildings of the town of
Tripoli, dominated by the great Tower of the Lions. They
were entering the wide bay in which the fleet was to anchor,
steering for its eastern shore. Dead ahead were the low,
rolling foothills, deep purple in colour and shimmering in
the intense heat; and beyond were the mountains of
Lebanon which had never been out of sight since they had
left Beirut.

Admiral Tryon turned to Lord Gillford to give him the
signal to reverse the direction of the fleet, which he had
outlined in his cabin. There was no single signal in the
book to cover the evolution Tryon had planned, and it had
to be made as two separate orders, one to each column.
Nor was it an evolution that could be carried out ex-
clusively by T.A. So at 3:25 precisely the yeoman bent
on the following:

Second Division alter course in succession 16 points to starboard, preserving the order of the fleet
and
First Division alter course in succession 16 points to port,
preserving the order of the fleet.

"Take the distance to the *Camperdown*," Lord Gillford
ordered a midshipman quickly. He had no intention of

questioning Tryon's order again, but this was an apparently innocent means of drawing his attention once more to the suicidally short distance between the two flagships.

"Six cables, sir," the midshipman reported promptly.

Six cables. Twelve hundred yards. The correct distance. And, as the lowest ordinary seaman knew, the combined turning circles of the *Victoria* and the *Camperdown* were not less than eight cables, or sixteen hundred yards. But if Tryon heard the midshipman's report he gave no sign of it, only turning in silence at the head of the companion ladder to ease his bulk down the rungs. Lord Gillford could do no more. Three times directly, and once indirectly, the commander-in-chief had been reminded that the distance between the columns was inadequate for the manœuvre he intended. As Captain Bourke suggested later, "Open criticism to one's superior is not quite consonant with true discipline," for that was "a dangerous course, striking deep at the foundations of discipline and responsibility."

Lord Gillford followed Tryon forward to the chart-house deck, a platform above the forebridge and conning tower, from which he customarily directed manœuvres when operating T.A. The time was 3:20. Already present there were Captain Bourke; Staff Commander Hawkins-Smith; Lieutenant Charles James Collins, the officer of the watch; Midshipman Herbert M. Lanyon, Bourke's *aide-de-camp;* and the yeoman of signals, J. Baggett. They saluted the admiral as he made his way to the rear rail, looking aft to see if all the ships of the first division had acknowledged the signal. Hawkins-Smith joined him, and the two officers talked together for some minutes, although what they discussed was never divulged, only that they had seemed to laugh.

Bourke had expected Tryon to remain on the after bridge. "I do not think I remember," he reported later, "a single case of his being forward at ordinary manœuvres." It was a particularly difficult situation for the flag captain, for he was still nominally in command of his ship and responsible for her safety, while Tryon was in command of the entire fleet and was responsible for the safety of every vessel in it. Yet Bourke knew that, within a few minutes, the order would have to be given for the helm of his ship to be put over in an evolution which, in his own mind, could have only one result. "My position," as he said later in his defence, "was one which I fancy very few, if any, have ever experienced in the service, especially in the presence of a master mind such as that of the commander-in-chief."

The Tripoli coastline was looming up ahead, and the fleet was approaching it at just under 9 knots. At 3:25 Tryon was reminded that it was time to turn. Two minutes later he was reminded again. Even in that time the vessels were a third of a mile closer to land. The greatest fleet in the world's greatest navy was heading straight for a foreign shore at 10 miles per hour, and with its gross momentum from some 100,000 tons of steel the need for a turn was becoming urgent. But before the helm could be put over, every battleship had to acknowledge the flagship's signal by repeating it "at the dip," and then to haul it close-up as a sign that it was understood. All but one of the ships of the two divisions appeared to have acknowledged and understood the order. Only the *Camperdown*, steaming a mere 1200 yards on the *Victoria*'s port beam, still showed her signal at the dip. "What are we waiting for?" Tryon asked impatiently, unaware of the *Camperdown*'s delay.

"I believe the *Camperdown*, sir," Lord Gillford told him.

"I'll just go aft and see if all the ships in our division have hauled up."

The *Camperdown!* There was Markham again, delaying an evolution by failing to acknowledge or apparently even to understand a simple signal! His only excuse could be that he had seen that one of the first division's battleships, whose yards were sometimes difficult to observe through the funnel smoke and obstructions from the *Victoria,* was still showing the signal at the dip. But Gillford came back within a few moments to reassure Tryon on that point.

"The *Camperdown* is the only ship we are waiting for, sir," Lord Gillford reassured him.

But the commander-in-chief had already acted in his absence, at 3:31, ordering the yeoman of signals to sema-phore to the *Camperdown:* "What are you waiting for?" and to show her pendants, an action which could only be inter-preted as a public rebuke. There was no more time to lose, as they were already well past the lines of bearing of their anchorage, and the shore was beginning to appear critically close.

At almost the same moment that the semaphore ceased its swift arm-swinging motions on the *Victoria*'s after bridge, the *Camperdown*'s repeat hoist was hauled close-up, showing that Markham and his flag captain had understood the order at last; and at once the *Victoria*'s signal was made executive by being hauled down.

"Go on to starboard,"[1] Tryon said at once, emphasizing his order, as was his custom, with a gesture.

"Hard astarboard—extreme helm," Hawkins-Smith called out to the helmsman. Within some thirty seconds the

---

[1] To turn to port the helm was starboarded; to turn to starboard, the helm was put to port.

Victoria began to turn, at first slowly, and then more swiftly, towards the *Camperdown;* and the *Camperdown* began her turn on a slightly wider arc towards the flagship.

Vice-Admiral Sir George Tryon was still standing at the after end of the chart-house deck as the manœuvre commenced, his gloved hands resting on the rail, looking astern of his ship to the *Nile* and the other battleships of his division to see that they put their helms over in succession as ordered. "An admiral's eyes should be aft and the captain's eyes forward," he had told Bourke so many times in the past. This was the crucial moment in an evolution, that would tax the skill of every subordinate, and he did not want to miss a single phase of it. The *Nile*'s helm was already hard over, and the great ship was turning, just inside the *Victoria*'s wake, her 12,000 tons heeling markedly in the dead calm sea.

The flagship's helm had turned through only two points when Bourke, who was close beside Tryon, desperately attempting to conceal his anxiety, said, "We had better do something, sir, we shall be too close to that ship"—indicating the *Camperdown.*

Tryon either ignored him or, as so often happened, was preoccupied with the exciting and critical moment of this complex evolution. This was the time when, like a choreographer watching the first rehearsal of a new ballet, he could observe the reality of the movement he had created in his mind. Even after his many years as a squadron or fleet commander, the fascination of witnessing the massive obedience and precision of these great turning ironclads could not have been wholly lost.

But Captain Bourke's obsession was with the *Camperdown,* fast approaching at a combined speed of almost eighteen knots and almost head-on. "Take the distance, Mr. Lanyon," he ordered the midshipman. And when the answer seemed delayed, he told him impatiently to hurry.

"Three and a quarter cables, sir," Lanyon replied at last; but Bourke thought this was an underestimate. The distance had been taken very hurriedly and only with an angle-board.

The next thirty seconds were critical—and less than two minutes had passed since the helm had been put over. If either of the closing flagships reversed its helm and reversed one screw, there was just a chance that a collision could still be prevented.

Again Bourke spoke to Tryon. "We had better do something, sir. We shall be very close to the *Camperdown*." And again there was no reply. "We are getting too close, sir! We must do something, sir!" Bourke appealed.

"May I go astern with the port screw?" Bourke asked, now in an agony of anxiety. Still there was no reply, although others on the chart-house deck who were farther off heard the urgent question. Twice more, and within thirty seconds, Bourke estimated later, he asked for the same permission.

And at last the admiral, who was standing by the chart box only a few feet from Bourke, turned from aft where he had continued to concentrate his attention closely on the *Nile*. He saw for the first time the terrifying proximity of the *Camperdown* and said at once, "Yes, go astern."

"Full speed astern port screw" Bourke called out. And then, this time without Tryon's permission, added, "Full speed astern both screws!"

Lieutenant Collins rushed into the chart house to put

the telegraph over, and the bells rang out in quick succession. Sixty feet below in the engine room the gongs echoed the order, and the triple expansion engines began the long, sustained labour of halting the progress through the water of the 11,000-ton ship they had been driving forward. But only four hundred yards separated the *Victoria* from the *Camperdown* now, and even their 14,000 horsepower could do little more than check the ironclad's progress before the two ships must meet.

There was nothing more to be done on board the *Victoria* to prevent a collision. Only the force of the impact could be reduced, and the responsibility for that rested solely on the reversed screws scrambling the water at the *Victoria's* stern into a frothing frenzy. It was the inevitability of the disaster that was hardest to bear. It added its own element of horror to the helplessness that every officer on the deck over the chart house felt, and they all succumbed to its power and the power of momentum that carried them towards the *Camperdown*. Only on the bridge below was the spell broken and initiative taken by one officer who kept his head.

"Pipe 'Close the watertight doors and out the collision mat,'" Lieutenant Herbert Heath (the acting executive officer, in the absence of Jellicoe) shouted to the boatswain's mate; and then, after failing to see the bugler, he ran down to the centre hatchway where he knew the Marines' messes were, trying to find someone who could give the alarm. But at that moment, above the continuous wail of the rapidly approaching *Camperdown's* foghorn, came the shrill sound of the upper-deck bugler sounding the "Gs."

Less than three minutes had passed since the helms of the two battleships had been put over. Now barely two

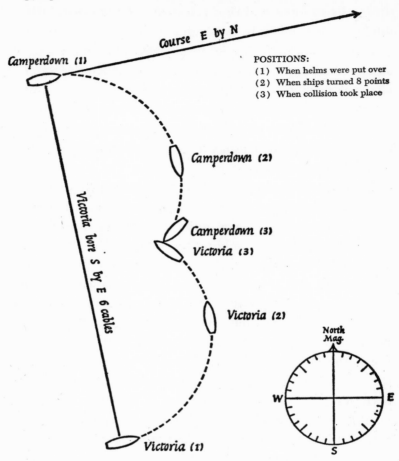

Course E by N

Camperdown (1)

POSITIONS:
(1) When helms were put over
(2) When ships turned 8 points
(3) When collision took place

Camperdown (2)

Victoria bore S by E 6 cables

Camperdown (3)
Victoria (3)

Victoria (2)

North Mag.

Victoria (1)

W   E

S

hundred yards separated them. Nor was the blow to be a glancing one, for the *Camperdown* had for some reason turned on a much wider arc than the *Victoria*, and at the point of intersection it appeared likely that her bow would strike the flagship on the starboard side at almost a right angle.

There were figures running on the upper and forecastle

decks of the *Victoria,* making for the collision mats that might staunch the flow of water through the hole still to be pierced by the *Camperdown's* ram. Above the continued blare of the bugle, which might have been urging the men into battle, there came the sound of their shouts and cries.

But above the chart house the state of numb paralysis persisted. There was no further sound, no movement, until the *Camperdown* was bearing down so close that the figures on her bridge could be identified, when Tryon suddenly paced across the deck and shouted through cupped hands in anguish to Markham, "Go astern—go astern!"

It was the only pathetic and futile order Sir George Tryon ever gave.

6

It seemed impossible such a thing could happen.
Captain J. W. Brackenbury
of H.M.S. Edinburgh

THE DECK OVER THE CHART HOUSE was ony a small area, some twelve feet across and no more than fifteen feet from aft to its curving triangular forward end, exposed to the elements and, in action, to every passing shell splinter. But on manœuvres it provided Tryon with a fine panoramic view of his fleet, visibility being obstructed only by the twin funnels just aft and the heavy mainmast beyond. The roof was bordered by pattern rails, and movement was restricted by the stays and shrouds and backstays of three small masts, two connected by a yard on which were worked the speed cone and flags. In addition, because of the extreme heat on that afternoon, an awning had been spread above as protection from the sun.

Contact between the ram of the *Camperdown* and the starboard side of the *Victoria* was made at 3:34 precisely, three and a quarter minutes after the helm of the *Victoria* had been put over. The speed of the *Camperdown*, approaching her flagship on a wider circle and almost at a right angle, was six knots, that of the *Victoria* rather over five knots. The *Camperdown* struck the *Victoria* about sixty-five feet from her bow, just forward from the turret; and with the *Camperdown*'s displacement weight of 10,600 tons and speed of six knots, the power of the blow was between 17,000 and 18,000 foot-tons; or equal to the impact of a blank shell from one of her 13.5-inch guns fired at the same range.

The *Camperdown's* hardened steel ram had been built onto her stem for the specific purpose of sinking ships in close combat, and it carried out its function for the first and last time with devastating efficiency, penetrating nine feet into the thin, unprotected bottom plating of the flagship. The stem tore into the carpenters' stores in the hold and the number one reserve coal bunker on the lower deck, buckling up and bursting the bulkhead between the bunker and the petty officers' mess, showering tons of best-quality Welsh coal over the tables and chairs and hammocks, scattering the men who had still not been completely awakened by the sound of the bugle a minute before, and breaking the leg of First Class Petty Officer Wheeler. He was picked up "perfectly black and covered in coal dust" by four of his bruised and shocked shipmates and rushed away towards the sick bay.

The stokers off duty heard only the splintering crash of the penetration, but on the adjoining mess deck the seamen still lying about on the floor or on their mess tables, knitting, sewing, or just dozing, suddenly heard a sound like an explosion and saw the broken stem of the *Camperdown* stationary in their midst, flanked by the raw, splintered steelwork of the ship's plates.

Elsewhere on the *Victoria* the impact was felt as no more than a sudden tremor, tending to cause those standing or walking to stumble, without being severe enough to throw anyone to the deck. This tremor sped like an earthquake's shock wave through storerooms, boiler rooms, engine rooms, and mess decks, through shell magazines and flats, bunkers and provision stores, down passages and aft two hundred feet to the wardroom, where tea was being taken.

Lieutenant George Loring, characteristically frugal in his use of colour, wrote home to his father, "It was a sort of push, and we heard a rending sound." Three hundred feet away and right aft in his cabin adjoining Captain Bourke's pantry, lying in his bunk with a temperature of 103 degrees, Commander John Jellicoe saw that "the foremost bulkhead of his cabin seemed to be wrenched, and looked as if it was going through the ship's side."

Up on the chart house, the officers and yeoman, and, behind them at the wheel, the quartermaster, clutched for the support of the rails or stays when the collision occurred. They all had a perfect view as the bows of the *Camperdown*, with her brass-decorated stem-piece glinting in the sun, bore down on them. During those last seconds her speed appeared far greater than her six knots, so fast and irresistible that it seemed as if she must slice clean through the *Victoria* and continue undisturbed on her way. Not until the stem touched and tore into the plating, bursting and splintering up the deck and setting it back in a heap of rubble towards amidships, did they duck their heads and shield their faces from the flying fragments of steel and wood and ironwork. When they looked again their ship had been thrust bodily some seventy feet to port and brought to a sudden standstill under a rising cloud of fine dust, and the *Camperdown*'s bow was locked deep into the fore part of the *Victoria*, filling the wound she had inflicted as neatly as a spear in flesh. The noise, for a brief second, had been tremendous, but had been stilled as suddenly as the *Camperdown*'s forward motion.

It was then, with the two flagships clutching each other

like gladiators at the moment of death, and the shock waves still perceptibly vibrating the deck, that the yeoman chose to pass Sir George Tryon a delayed semaphore just received from the *Camperdown,* in answer to the flagship's demand to know what she was waiting for.

"Because I did not quite understand your signal," the message read.

Tryon glanced down at this last message, this last excuse he would receive from his second-in-command, grabbed a hailer, and put it to his lips. "Go astern, go astern with both engines. Why didn't you—?" he called across to Markham, standing among his bunched officers on the *Camperdown*'s forebridge less than fifty yards away.

But the sound of his voice was lost in the noise of the machinery hoisting out the boats on the *Camperdown,* and though Markham came to the port side of his bridge at the suggestion of his staff, he did not hear even Tryon's opening words.

However, the order had already been complied with, and now that the *Camperdown* had been halted by the collision, the engines had only to thrust into reverse her 10,000 tons and free her bows from the jagged grip in which the *Victoria* held her. In less than a minute the *Camperdown*'s backward motion was perceptible. Accompanied by a fearful grinding of steel against steel, she slowly eased her way out of the roughly triangular cavity, which had been torn even wider as the sterns of the two battleships tended to swing together. Within two minutes she was free; and, like a torrent over the wreckage of a burst dam, the water began to roar and foam in at a rate of hundreds of tons a minute. At once the *Victoria* settled forward and heeled slowly to starboard.

"I think I had better go below to see about the doors," Bourke said quickly.

"Yes, you go below to look after the doors," Tryon agreed. "I will attend to the engines." And Captain Bourke leaped down on to the fore-and-aft bridge and ran aft.

Tryon appeared calm and under control again. The ship was badly damaged but quite clearly not in imminent danger of sinking. But for reassurance he turned to the staff commander. "Do you think she'll continue to float?" he asked.

"I think she ought to keep afloat as the damage is so far forward," Hawkins-Smith told him. "Shall we steer for the land to try to beach her, sir?"

"What water are we in?"

"Deep water, seventy to eighty fathoms."

Tryon glanced to port and saw the *Nile*, very close and almost dead ahead. "Yes, go astern with the port engine, ahead with the starboard, and point her clear of the *Nile*."

"What speed, sir? Full?" Hawkins-Smith asked.

"No, go seven knots."

The revolution telegraph was put at 38, and the bells rang out in the chart house.

Lord Gillford, still awaiting orders beside Tryon, had been watching the other ships of the fleet, which gave greater evidence of anxiety than that shown by the admiral and his staff commander.

"The *Dreadnought*'s lowering boats, sir," the flag lieutenant reported. Nor was she the only ship taking emergency action.

"Make a signal to annul sending boats." Tryon spoke angrily. He had not ordered the boats out. There was no question of the ship's going down. She was one of the newest, finest, and most heavily protected ironclads in the Royal Navy, the flagship of the Mediterranean Fleet. Below decks she was honeycombed with watertight compartments, and these were being closed now under the supervision of petty officers and officers and the ship's captain himself. Besides, as Hawkins-Smith had stressed, the blow had been struck well forward of the ship's vitals. The *Victoria* was safe for the present.

Below the chart house, Lieutenant Herbert Heath and a party of men were struggling to get the large collision mat onto the forecastle and over the side. If this form of first-aid dressing, which had saved so many damaged ships in the past, could be placed over the hole, it would staunch the inflow of water. But it was a heavy, awkward piece of equipment, and the men's movements were obstructed by ropes and stays, rails and capstans, lockers and screens, and then by the wreckage itself. They shouted instructions to one another, swore and stumbled and fought to heave it over the twelve-foot gash.

To the anxious audience above it was a brief drama that could have only one ending. Within two minutes of the *Camperdown*'s breaking clear, the calm sea was lapping over onto the deck far forward, reaching out towards the open chain lockers and ripped-up decking. Its rate of advance was swifter than any tide, and accelerated at every second, so that men who felt it about their ankles at one moment were wading the next. It was a hopeless struggle, and one by one they retreated through the swirling water, gasping and clutching for support, and leaving the unrolled mat awash.

Tryon had been watching them with helpless exaspera-
tion, and when he saw their surrender he shouted down,
"Close the apertures!"

But it was already too late for that. The sea was surging
over onto the upper deck, gushing down the bitts, the
chain hatches, the windlass cover, adding to the flood in
the compartments below. Side scuttles, gun ports, vents—
everything that might cool the interior of the ship on that
burning afternoon had been left open. It was even too late
to prevent the water from pouring through the huge turret
apertures of the 16.25-inch guns; and as the vessel heeled
even more steeply to starboard, the intake of water accelerated, so that within five minutes of the collision the bows
had already sunk some fifteen feet.

The forecastle was clear of men now. From the chart
house they could be seen standing about uncertainly, drip-
ping wet and panting from their exertions, watching the
advancing swirl of water like flood survivors on a river
bank. But why weren't the compartments holding?
Hawkins-Smith had been right. The *Victoria* should have
been able to withstand a worse blow than this so near to
her bows. And the water could not yet have reached the
boilers, for the rhythm of the engines could still be felt,
and the ship was moving forward on her tight circle.

But she was moving very sluggishly, so slowly that Tryon
asked Hawkins-Smith if by any chance the anchor had gone,
falling over four hundred feet to grip the ocean bed.

"No, sir, it's in its place, not touched."

The *Victoria* was in no condition to travel at more than
a few knots and would never attain the seven knots Tryon
had stipulated. It was a wonder that she was moving at all.
She was carrying an additional load of some two thousand

tons, and her bows were now far out of sight beneath the sea. Even the muzzles of her great guns were brushing the surface of the water, and their turret was almost a circular island. It was like trying to manœuvre a waterlogged barge; but she was nearly round on her new course.

"Helm amidships," Hawkins-Smith ordered the quartermaster. The ship was heading towards the land, four and a half miles distant, engines still at thirty-eight revolutions, but speed no more than three knots.

The quartermaster attempted without success to right the helm. "I cannot move the helm, sir," he called back to Hawkins-Smith helplessly. "The pressure's off." Nor could Hawkins-Smith make any impression on the wheel when he pushed the quartermaster aside and heaved at it. It was held fast.

Was this the first sign of the breakdown of the flagship's machinery? Already the hydraulics had gone. It would be the telegraphs next, and then the engines. . . .

"Ring down to the engine room and tell them to keep it on," Hawkins-Smith ordered. With no hydraulic pressure none of the larger boats could be launched. It was essential that they should not lose this source of power.

The heel was close to twenty degrees and it was becoming difficult even to stand without support. The sea was lapping the fore battery ports, which, like everything else on the ship, were still wide open. In another minute it would be sweeping past the 6-inch guns onto the ship's main deck, down into the main passage, into the main magazine and shell room. Already the ship's appearance was grotesque, so frighteningly unnatural that it seemed impossible that she could stay afloat.

Even Tryon recognized that the *Victoria*'s end was near.

Some human or mechanical failure must have occurred below decks to allow the sea to flood in at this terrifying rate, breaking into compartment after compartment, so that within eight minutes of the collision the whole fore part of the vessel was filled and her stern was so high that the screws were almost free.

"I think she's going," he said to the staff commander.

"Yes, sir, I think she is," Hawkins-Smith agreed.

Tryon turned next to Lord Gillford behind him. "Make a signal to send boats immediately," he told him. He was quite cool, and his voice had lost its note of belligerence.

Only the yeoman was left, and the quartermaster, still angrily trying to right the helm like a child with a broken toy. There was an air of desertion up here, high above the upper deck and swamped forecastle. But on the narrow fore-and-aft bridge just below, sixteen-year-old Midshipman Lanyon was still awaiting orders.

"Don't stay there, youngster, go to a boat," Tryon told him.

But before the boy could move, the *Victoria* gave a sudden heavy lurch to starboard. It was not yet 3:44, little more than nine minutes since the *Camperdown* had struck.

The ship's company below decks at the time of the collision were divided between those few who were immediately aware of the critical damage and the many hundreds more who only felt the shudder of impact and heard the bugle calling them to collision stations. The men who were nearest to the breach and who witnessed the first terrifying inrush of water were hurriedly retreating, slamming shut and bolting the compartment doors and hatches behind them, and the news travelled spasmodically in sudden cries

Vice-Admiral Sir George Tryon, K.C.B.

Rear Admiral Albert Hastings Markham

H.M.S. *Victoria*

H.M.S. *Camperdown*

Captain the Honourable Archibald Maurice Bourke

Lieutenant Lord Gillford

Staff Commander Thomas Hawkins-Smith

Vice-Admiral Sir Michael Culme-Seymour

The sinking flagship

Men escaping over the stern of H.M.S. *Victoria*

Boats to the rescue

The court martial on H.M.S. *Hibernia*

down passages and gangways. But aft there was at first no sense of crisis. There had been a collision—they all knew that. And they had their posts to go to and their duties to perform. But, as they lacked the visual evidence of the men forward, their situation, for the present, appeared secure.

Far below, in the boiler rooms, stokeholds, and engine rooms, the stokers, artificers, and engineers were the last to hear that they were holed; and, though they were all conscious of the increasing heel of their ship, they never knew until the last sudden lurch that she was going down. When Bourke arrived in the starboard engine and boiler rooms after being sent below by Tryon, he found the men working in their hot, dim world of coal dust, oil, and glinting bearings as if the flagship were still steaming at the head of her fleet, and he heard the telegraph gongs ringing out above the beat of the machinery.

"No, there's no water here," Engineer Deadman told Bourke in answer to his inquiry. Bourke hurried on, unescorted for this emergency inspection. In the darkness of the starboard flats the doors were closed and the scuttles shut, and the air was heavy with the sense of disaster. Dim figures were running past, in ordered but hurried retreat. "Is everything tight?" Bourke called out, and an unidentified voice answered, "Yes."

The bolts had been screwed home in the doors to the forward mess deck, and there was no escape for anyone caught beyond them. But the water was still pouring in, from where it was impossible to tell in the half-light. There was no one about, and the only sound came from the steady, wicked inrush of the sea. Below in the submerged flat a party was struggling with the big horizontal door, and another group responsible for the doors further aft "had not even time to close some of their doors properly, the water was bursting in so fast," Bourke reported later. Men were already dying, minutes before the ship went down, some drowned in the flood or bowled over and stunned in its rush, or, most terribly of all, trapped behind doors feverishly bolted and clipped home by their shipmates. None of the stoker double-bottom party was picked up later, and this was probably their fate. One man who "thought he was done for" when the turret escape hatch was slammed on him beat it with such force with his fists that it was opened again to let him through; and Captain James Lumsden still remembers, sixty-five years after the event, that terror of being left behind in the darkness, "but I luckily heard movement behind me and just got through the doors as they were being closed."

Bourke ran next along the main passage and in the dim light bumped into Fleet Engineer Felix Foreman. "Is everything shut down?" Bourke panted out.

"Everything's tight as far as I can make out abaft the foremost boiler room," Foreman replied. He was in a state of obvious distress, uncertain of what he was doing. Bourke had met him earlier on his flying inspection, and Foreman had told his captain that he did not know where he was.

But Bourke had seen and heard enough to know that his ship was doomed and that it must be abandoned at once. From the main passage he hurried up onto deck to see if everything was being done to get out the boats, in spite of the loss of hydraulic power, and then forward to report to Tryon. On the way he met Lieutenant Heath, who had also been below after failing with the collision mat, and he, like his captain, had seen "the water coming in in great volumes forward."

"Fall in the men on the port side of the quarter deck,"
Bourke called out to him, and leaped up the ladder to the
fore-and-aft bridge. From here he could see that his order
had been anticipated. There were his men below, some six
hundred of them, fallen in four deep, Bourke related later,
turned amidships, their backs to the ship's side as if on
parade. "Some officer gave the order, which was repeated
by the master-at-arms, who was near, and who will be able
to corroborate this statement. 'Right about turn,' and the
whole ship's company turned to the right about and faced
the ship's side."

The discipline was superb. Every man present, swim-
mer and non-swimmer alike, knew that within seconds
he would be cast into the sea, but not one of them broke
ranks, except two Maltese bumboatmen, both canteen
workers and not Navy men, who suddenly threw themselves
over the rail with a cry.

Above the tight, silent crowd, a man was calling out,
"Steady, men, steady." He was the Reverend Samuel Mor-
ris, ship's chaplain, a Welshman, who was to become the
symbol of heroism on the *Victoria*. Already nearing his
sixtieth year, "this noble, beloved character," as Bourke
called him, had seen service in all parts of the world since
leaving his post as second master at Ystrad Meurig Grammar
School, high up in the hills of Cardigan. His was a won-
derfully calming influence during those final tense seconds,
and "even at the moment of capsizing we only hear of him,
careless of his own safety, exhorting the men to be cool."

Then came that last lurch, and the whole ship's company
recognized that the end had come. "Jump! Jump!" Lieutenant Heath shouted at the top of his voice from the after
bridge.

Two groups of the ship's personnel who required special attention were the sick and the prisoners. Surgeon Ellis naturally went first to the commander's cabin, where he found Jellicoe being attended by his servant, who was helping him into his coat over his pyjamas. He was in good hands, appeared steadier on his feet than a man with his temperature should have been, and required no further attention. Ellis next darted into Tryon's spare cabin and told Midshipman Gambier that he would be back again if necessary, and made his way to the sick bay. There were no serious cases left, only one fever victim, who was dressing and seemed able to look after himself, so he ran up onto deck to see what the state of affairs was, "and to tell Surgeon Minter to try to collect the sick into one party." Then, "thinking things were getting serious," Ellis ran down to Gambier again. The midshipman was very weak and had little chance unless he could be got into a boat.

"Hurry up and carry him up to the quarter deck and get him onto a chair," Ellis told the Marine servant who was trying to pull Gambier's trousers over his pyjamas.

On the quarter deck he was told that all the sick were together now, and that there was one man whose leg was broken, the petty officer caught by the avalanche of coal on the ship's impact with the *Camperdown*. Two or three minutes later Ellis could still see no signs of Gambier, and once again he clambered down the ladders to the cabin, "but when I got there the cabin was empty, and I suppose that he was carried up another ladder, probably, so that we crossed."

The ship's prisoners were easier to attend to. There were only two, and their cells were promptly unlocked by

the police and they were escorted up onto deck by the
sentry. Unlike Midshipman Gambier, the wounded petty
officer, and so many of the sick, they were to survive.

The *Victoria* and *Camperdown,* by turning in towards
each other, were only initiating an evolution in which the
other nine vessels in the two divisions had been ordered to
follow "in succession." In theory, then, if each captain had
carried out his instructions and followed the movements of
the guide of his division, collisions would have followed at
roughly two-minute intervals between the ships of the
first division and their opposite numbers in the second
division. Later the captains had an opportunity of describing their personal reactions to the situation and the steps
they took to avoid such a nicely spaced series of disasters.
Some claimed to have understood from the beginning what
they imagined their commander-in-chief had in mind;
others that, though they were puzzled, they never for one
moment were in danger of collision. This may have been
true of the last ships in the columns; it certainly did not
apply to the *Nile,* the *Dreadnought,* and the *Inflexible* of
the first division, or to the *Edinburgh* of the second division,
a particularly unhandy vessel, which had begun its turn
behind the *Camperdown* and righted its helm just in time
to pass astern of Markham's flagship.

"It never entered my head that I should ram the *Victoria,*"
Noel of the *Nile* reported later. But his starboard bow
missed her by only some one hundred yards as he swung
round with full helm and reversed port screw, and his stern
swung to within fifty yards of the flagship. Witnesses on
the *Victoria* put the distance at half that figure. Brackenbury of the *Edinburgh* could not report how many points

he had turned when he saw that a collision was inevitable, because "my attention was taken up in getting my ship out of danger, and I did not look at the compass." The *Inflexible*'s captain stopped both engines, sheered out to starboard, and then drifted to port, finishing up some two hundred yards from the *Victoria*. Captain Arthur William Moore of the *Dreadnought* "ordered the helm hard-a-starboard, full speed astern with the port engine, and when the head of the ship was clear of the *Nile*, full speed astern both, and stopped her way."

These emergency measures, by skill and good fortune, prevented further catastrophe. But they could not prevent the two divisions from lapsing into a state of chaos more frightful and humiliating than anything the proud Mediterranean Fleet had ever known. But to the credit of the commanding officers, every ship had her boats hoisted out before they had heaved to. On some of the battleships the alarm had been given even before the collision occurred, and by the time the *Camperdown* had reversed clear of the flagship, every man in the fleet, except those on watch below, was on deck or racing up the ladders.

Midshipman Hugh Tweedie described the moment of alarm on the *Dreadnought*[1] when every one of the occupants of the gunroom was asleep, some on, some under the table, others on the settee. The gunroom was ventilated by an opening on to the quarter deck, and down this a head was thrust and a voice was heard shouting, "Away all boats to the *Victoria!*" A stampede followed, Tweedie breaking clear to take his place on the second whaler. On a dozen mess decks and in the offices' wardrooms the

[1] *The Story of a Naval Life,* by Admiral Sir Hugh Tweedie, K.C.B.

scene was repeated as the bugles rang out and the alarm was called. In the *Collingwood*'s gunroom, where they were having seven-bells tea, a snottie came tearing in, shouting, "The old *Victoria*'s made a mess of it," and the boys stepped into their shoes, grabbed their caps, and ran.

The first acute excitement on the vessels scattered about the crippled flagship changed to a sudden anxiety when the seriousness of the incident was appreciated. This was no lark, no minor *gaffe* by Bertie Markham such as had occurred before and been the subject of an evening's gossip. It was soon clear that they were witnessing a calamity more terrible than anything any of the officers or men present had ever before experienced. Visibility was perfect, the sea still dead calm, and none of the thousands of onlookers was as much as half a mile away from the scene. Those who were not already on deck had missed the concussion of the collision, which had followed the sudden cloud from the *Victoria*'s forecastle—a cloud that might have been caused by a direct shell hit. But everyone saw the two flagships locked together, then their painfully slow separation, and the sudden heel of the *Victoria* as if a supporting prop under her starboard bow had been removed. Even the men manning the fleet's boats and rowing frantically towards the flagship caught glimpses, if only intermittently over their shoulders, of the forecastle party on the *Victoria* struggling with the collision mat, knee-deep in water. Then, as they rested anxiously on their oars or rowed reluctantly back at the "annul sending boats" signal from the flagship, they saw her turn laboriously with the seas washing clear over her bows and rising at a terrifying speed up the forecastle and round the forward main gun turret. "The suspense was agonizing and we could hardly bear it," one midshipman said later; and many of the rescue crews disobeyed an admiral's order for the first time in their lives and continued towards the *Victoria,* even before she began to turn over.

The *Collingwood* was "duty steamboat" that afternoon, so her launch had steam up already. Her captain, the big, heavily bearded "Abe" Jenkins, had her out and launched within a minute of the *Camperdown's* clearing the flagship, and the boom boats out seconds later. He seemed to be in no doubt from the first that the *Victoria* was finished, hailed his crews to keep going in spite of the negative boats order, and as a consequence picked up more survivors than any other ship.

Captain Noel on the bridge of the *Nile,* and only a hundred yards from the *Victoria,* was in a better position than anyone else to observe her capsizing, which, according to Bourke, was "almost momentary. She seemed to turn over in an incredibly short space of time." Like every other witness, Noel was appalled at the speed of the flagship's end, and at the manner of her going. Neither he nor any of his officers on the *Nile's* bridge expected her to reach the shore. They thought that she would continue to heel, and then, like any holed ship in a calm sea, slowly—very slowly —dip down beneath the water, by which time most of her company would have got away in their own boats, leaving perhaps a few to be picked up. To lose a new battleship— and the flagship of the Mediterranean Fleet—would be a great enough calamity, and no doubt there would be a few casualties even under these favourable circumstances. But there was not an officer or man present who could have foreseen the fearful events that followed that last lurch when the *Victoria* was still heading for the Tripoli shore, heeling over at twenty degrees and with a third of her length beneath the sea.

"Without any other warning," Noel related, "she appeared to fall over to starboard, slowly at first but with increasing rapidity." The *Victoria* was capsizing, spinning about her axis like some great waterlogged piece of debris, and "as she went over, the boats and weight on the port side fell to leeward with a terrible crash. The ship then turned keel up, and with her bow depressed at about an angle of 20 to 30 degrees," she slipped down, leaving only her extreme stern and the still revolving blades of her propellers exposed before disappearing.

Her last lurch, her sudden capsizing were so violent that her end came rather as an explosion than as the usual turbulent disappearance of a sinking ship. The air from her interior had no time to escape as she went down, and burst forth from her bowels, throwing up the lashed gunnery targets and other remaining loose objects on her upper decks and a great mass of material from below. From the bridge of the *Victoria*'s sister ship, the *Sans Pareil*, Captain A. K. Wilson watched in horror through a glass. "A great rush of air came from the stern ports," he described it, "and as the water entered the funnels as she was turning over there was something like an explosion of steam, apparently due to the water getting into the furnaces. After she sank, large quantities of air came up, keeping the centre over where the ship had gone down clear, and spreading the men and wreckage in a circle around."

At the *sauve qui peut*, the thick, disciplined ranks of some six hundred bluejackets assembled on the port side of the

Victoria broke up like a flock of roosting birds at a gunshot, and were seen flying through the air, one after another, more and still more, dozens at a time, turning over and over before tumbling into the sea below. Many more, who were unable to swim or who were alarmed at the frightening distance of the water, held back at the rails and only leaped in panic as the ship began to rotate, landing in the water, swimmers and non-swimmers together, tightly bunched. Others scrambled over the rails and along the side when she was at ninety degrees, and then onto her bottom as she rotated farther, like lumberjacks spinning an outsize river log. Many more just waited for the sea to carry them away, and of these some were caught up in the mast stays and cross-stays, the awning that was spread aft, or one or another of the hundreds of ropes and wires and struts and other obstructions spread about and over the upper deck. Farther aft, and too close to the ship's stern, more men broke clear and dropped down from the dizzy height above the admiral's sternwalk, where the port propeller was "churning up the water and playing havoc with the poor fellows who had got within the sweep of the blades."[1]

But there had been no order to the men on watch below, in the boiler rooms and engine rooms, to leave their posts. They were still there, in the hold, when the ship capsized and started to go down, her engines still audibly beating out their rhythm under water, down four hundred and fifty feet until she struck her bows against the bottom and fell back sluggishly in a cloud of ocean mud onto the sea bed. Not one of them was saved.

[1] Riley.

At 3:30 the Mediterranean Fleet had been sailing on an east-by-north course in precise and stately formation, three miles from its anchorage. Fifteen minutes later it was milling about in a condition of utter pandemonium. Markham's flagship was down at the bows and in danger of sinking, and all that remained of Tryon's flagship was a sprinkling of debris and hundreds of bobbing heads, all surging out concentrically before the single huge wave that washed clean the sea's surface and left only a widening circle of foam and bubbles, like a giant saucepan of boiling milk. Nothing could live there, and Markham hailed the rescue boats making for it to steer clear. The wave was a moving frontier between the living and the dead, between those who had been "drawn down in the suck" and those swept out to where there was at least a chance of survival. It was also an arbitrary frontier, without distinction between strong swimmers and weak swimmers and those who could not swim at all.

That fatal wave took time to expend itself, some said as long as five minutes, and when it was gone, to be replaced by a less violent and more general turbulence, the shocked and helpless onlookers among the remaining scattered battleships saw that there were many fewer heads left above the water awaiting rescue from the boats darting among them. "It seemed too dreadful to realize," Captain Brackenbury of the *Edinburgh* wrote in a letter. "It seemed impossible such a thing could happen; and yet there we all were, all motionless round the spot, where a few broken pieces of wood marked the place where the *Victoria* was. . . . The scene haunts one to this moment."

The *Victoria*'s captain of the forecastle was one of those who took the dangerous route over the stern into the sea. After failing to place the collision mat he had fallen in with the rest of the company and had darted aft at the cry of "Jump!" He leaped down onto the rear gun mounting, over the rail, and down the hull, slipping and breaking his thigh against the shaft casing, a few feet from the whirling blades. Then he fell helplessly between the propeller shaft and the ship's bottom, kicking himself clear with his good leg as the stern sank beside him. Chief Petty Officer Dick May was another who escaped this way. He got onto the sternwalk with Tryon's steward as the *Victoria* gave her last lurch, and grabbed the lifebuoy that always hung there. "My God, Jack, she's gone!" he exclaimed to the steward, and at once jumped out as far as he could, clearing the screws. He stayed with the lifebuoy until he was picked up, and later sent this admiral's safeguard to the bereaved Lady Tryon as a memento of the occasion. The steward was less fortunate, and may have been one of those cut to pieces.

The thought of those racing screws was the dominating fear among many of the officers and men, and they did do great slaughter. Lieutenant Loring went down a long way with the ship, retaining his hold on a rope he had clutched at the last second "for fear of the screws above me." But they did not kill as many men as the wooden debris that was torn from the *Victoria* as she went down, and even after she lay on the bottom. That, said Loring, "was the worst part of the whole thing." Fragments of boats and gratings, a mass of timber that had been used as gunnery targets, derricks and furniture from the mess decks and cabins, "all sorts of floatable articles came up with tremendous force, and the surface of the water was one seething mass. We were whirled round and round, and half choked with water, and dashed about amongst the wreckage until half senseless."

Captain Bourke described it as "this enormous swirl of water carrying with it spars and wreckage and things which came up to injure and kill the swimmers, none of them knowing what hit them, or how they were hit, but only that they were hit." Even some of the rescue boats were put in danger from this extraordinary storm, and one of the first on the scene was nearly stove in by the *Victoria*'s main derrick, fifty feet long and weighing several tons, which shot out of the ocean like a frenzied serpent.

But more deadly than either the screws or the debris was the huge circular wave that dragged the men in the water down and tossed some of them up again, or threw them into the vortex about the descending hull of the battleship. After being "precipitated head first down the side of the ship" and being washed off, Gunner Frederick John Johnson was "sucked down a great distance, and on reaching the surface I could really count between thirty and forty heads round me." Twice more he went down under that wave, "and on coming to the surface I struck my head against some wreckage." When he looked about him again "there were only three or four people."

With the breaking of the ranks on the *Victoria*'s upper deck, the sick became scattered, and those who were able to looked after themselves as well as they could. Judged on the numerous examples of heroism and unselfishness among the ship's company in the water, it is unlikely that any men as ill as Midshipman Gambier were left to fend for themselves. Some from the sick bay lived to describe the holocaust in the water. Commander John Jellicoe was still struggling weakly with a party of men to hoist out one of the boom boats after the hydraulics had gone when the *Victoria* began to turn over. "We had better go down the side of the ship as she turns over," he said to Gunnery Lieutenant Arthur Leveson. "We started to walk down the port side," he wrote later, "which by that time was horizontal. . . . I held on to the jackstay as the hull turned over." Then Jellicoe let go, "feeling the suction of her sinking, but was not drawn down . . . and conscious of bodies passing me." When he reached the surface he struck out and swam rapidly away, but soon felt the weakness of his fevered limbs. His life was probably saved by Midshipman Philip Roberts-West, who found him in an exhausted state and asked if he could give a hand. "I said I would be glad if I might put a hand on his shoulder. . . ." Within ten minutes the commander and the boy were picked up by one of the *Nile*'s boats. The swim appeared to have done Jellicoe no harm, for the next day his temperature was normal. Not far away, Hugh Tweedie of the *Dreadnought* chanced on a chest of drawers which he tried to drag into his whaler. But it was too heavy, and when he stove it in with an oar to save the contents, the clothes he dragged out were marked "Commander J. Jellicoe."

Lieutenant Herbert Heath, after giving the order to jump, found himself "absolutely flying through the air." He came up in an area crowded thick with struggling men, where, in the condition they were in, the non-swimmers "may have taken good swimmers down with them." Many of these non-swimmers were middle-aged stokers and Marines and even able seamen with many years' service,

who prided themselves on never getting a foot wet. Lord
Gillford was almost taken down by one of these strong,
desperate men, who could never be assisted and only
threshed about wildly, grabbing for anything, before going
down; and Fleet Surgeon Ellis became involved with this
"mass of men who were so close together that one could
not strike out."

Captain Bourke never reached Tryon to give his report
on the state of the ship. He was halfway along the port
side of the fore-and-aft bridge when the *Victoria* began to
capsize, and was at once taken down. "Then, just after I
came up to the surface, all I recollect was seeing just a
small portion of the stern sticking up, and the screws
sticking out of the water a very considerable distance off."

"The Commander-in-Chief and myself were on top of the
chart house at the last," wrote Hawkins-Smith in his official
report. He went down far with the ship, before fighting
clear of the rope and wire and canvas awning that caged in
the top of the chart house and made it a death-trap in an
emergency. Even when he was free, the ship's suction
caught him. "And then I saw a dark shadow over me, which
I believe to have been the ship, but striking out away from
it, I eventually came up so exhausted, that had I not found
close to me, on reaching the surface, an oar and small spar,
which I placed under each arm, I would certainly have been
drowned."

But Tryon made no attempt to save himself, and it is
doubtful if he ever escaped from the entanglement surrounding him. He was last seen, in correct accord with
tradition, his hands on the rail, awaiting the end; and he
made no remark that might have revealed his feelings
during those final seconds. "He was perfectly calm and

collected to the last," Hawkins-Smith wrote later. "He went down, and was seen by no one again; and I never expected to see him, as I am sure he, being a short-breathed man, could not have kept the water out of his lungs as long as I was able to do, and I could not have done so a second or two longer. . . . He died as he had lived, a brave man."

7

Jack saved. An awful affair. Thank God.
*Commander John Jellicoe in a telegram to his
father, a retired captain, in the Isle of Wight*

LIKE ANY GREAT CALAMITY, the sinking of the *Victoria* created its own legends. The story ran throughout the fleet, and was believed by many, that hundreds of excited and expectant Syrians witnessed the collision from the hills overlooking Tripoli Bay. The sight was merely the reward for a day's vigil, a local fakir having prophesied a week earlier that "Allah had determined to visit the ships of the infidels." The form of retribution had not been decreed, but they went home satisfied before sundown. It was also said that two hours after the collision, a huge crowd had gathered at the gates of the Malta dockyard. Word of some great disaster had somehow got about on the island even before the fleet finally anchored at Tripoli, and without the aid of wireless telegraphy. Back in England, Lieutenant Reginald H. Bacon and a number of fellow officers were lunching that day at the Whitehead torpedo works at Weymouth. With lunch over, and the discussion continuing on the subject of the morning's work observing torpedo trials, one of the officers' wine glasses suddenly broke at the stem of its own accord. "That should mean a big naval disaster," one of the officers remarked lightly; and it was not until later that they recalled independently that the *Victoria* had gone down at that precise moment. Then there was the

most famous story of all, the story of Lady Tryon's reception, repeated all over the country at the time and still told
in naval circles today. The London season was at its height,
and Lady Tryon was "at home" to some two hundred people
at her Eaton Squire house. A number of guests as they were
received remarked to their hostess how pleasant it was for
her to have her husband home again so soon. "But he is still
in the Mediterranean," Lady Tryon told them at first in
surprise and later in some vexation. But many people had
seen Sir George, quite distinctly, coming down the stairs
to welcome them, and some even claimed to have greeted
him.

Among the survivors and witnesses of the disaster, stark
and terrible reality was at first enough, although the
mythology of the *Victoria*'s end later became prodigious in
the Mediterranean Fleet. But one curious and disturbing
story began at once to circulate among the lower decks,
originating among the survivors and confirmed by many
of the onlookers. The most horrifying incident had been
the sudden capsizing of the flagship, and the cause of this
was, apparently, the tearing away of the *Victoria*'s 111-ton
guns and turret, which, with their heavy armour and mounting, must have weighed in all some 2000 tons. When the
ship was at its extreme angle of heel, witness after witness
testified, the guns had swung in their turret and broken
away from their mountings, dragging the ship down with
them. Not one officer could be found to confirm this story,
which was not only rejected at the later inquiry but deemed
to be a technical impossibility. But those huge guns had
created their own myth years before, ever since the time of
the first test firings, when men went sick rather than be
present at their posts in the turret, and the gunnery petty

officer responsible was sometimes too nervous to press the
button. There was something almost supernatural about
their very size. Nobody trusted them, especially after their
early record, and with the memory of the *Thunderer* incident still fresh in everyone's mind. Everyone wanted a
conclusive explanation, and this one was not only unanswer-
able but had a satisfying touch of the macabre about it.

This was the story that was being related by survivors
to their rescuers even before the last boat had been hoisted
back aboard, an hour after the *Victoria* went down. The
other topic, while the whalers and launches ran to and fro
across the still-agitated waters above the *Victoria,* search-
ing for bodies among the wreckage, was the appearance of
the *Camperdown.* For a time her condition looked as serious
as that of the flagship shortly before she had gone down.
The sea was over her bow and halfway up to her forward
barbette, and her after gangways were well out of the water.
Markham was certain that she was going to follow the
Victoria to the bottom. But after some ninety minutes of
hard pumping, divers were able to get down to the vital
half-closed bulkhead door to secure it. But seven compartments were still flooded when she gave the signal to form
up and leave for the anchorage, and she looked a pitiful
sight as she led the Mediterranean Fleet in towards Tripoli
at quarter-speed. As a deep red sun went down over Tripoli
Bay and a damp evening coolness descended over the
anchored ships, diving parties left in boats for the flagship;
and all night the men worked on the *Camperdown*'s bows
to repair the twisted, broken stem-piece and patch the six-
by-ten-foot jagged hole.

At the extreme stern of the *Camperdown,* some three
hundred feet distant from the divers and engineers, Mark-

ham, his flag lieutenant, and staff, with Captain Johnstone and the senior officers of the ship, sat down in conference in the admiral's cabin. Clearly it must have been an anxious and defensive meeting, each member cautious in his choice of words and aware that every statement and opinion made now would be recorded and remembered by those present, just as every command given and carried out during the afternoon would later be made known to the world. "There must be more than one on the *Camperdown* who is tempted to regret that he did not go below on the *Victoria* yesterday," the London correspondent of the *New York Times* was to write the following day.

It would not be fair to suggest that this was the attitude that prevailed in Markham's cabin that evening. But guilt and fear must have been present. Captain Johnstone had just discovered that Markham's order to go full speed astern as the *Camperdown* bore down on the *Victoria* had not been correctly carried out. Commander William Marwood Daniell knew that he would soon have to explain, to higher authority than his rear admiral, why he had not even been on deck during the crucial manœuvre. The chief engineer knew that there would be the closest questioning on the failure to shut the watertight doors. And Rear Admiral Markham himself understood with fearful clarity that he would be called upon by the Admiralty to show how his flagship had sunk a first-class battleship, and drowned 358 officers and men, among them the most esteemed admiral in the Royal Navy—"our gallant and ever-to-be-lamented Chief," as he wrote of him in his diary the following day. It is also certain that none of these officers had experience to draw on that might help them in such a situation.

There was an appalling amount of work to be done in a short time: a casualty list had to be prepared, arrangements made to transport the sick and other survivors to Malta, the funeral and burial details attended to, and a fresh schedule of operations for the fleet had to be drawn up. Finally, and most urgently, the wording of an initial telegram to the Admiralty reporting the disaster, and a full report on the day's operations, had to be discussed.

Half an hour after midnight the following telegram was dispatched to the Secretary of the Admiralty, Sir Ughtred Kay-Shuttleworth, through the British Consul at Tripoli and the Foreign Office:

Regret to report whilst manœuvring this afternoon off Tripoli *Victoria* and *Camperdown* collided. *Victoria* sank fifteen minutes after in 80 fathoms. Bottom uppermost. *Camperdown* struck *Victoria* before the turret starboard. Following officers drowned: . . .

The list included, besides Sir George Tryon, the names of one lieutenant; the fleet paymaster; the fleet engineer, Felix Foreman; four more engineers; the ship's chaplain; seven midshipmen, and others making up a total of twenty-two officers.

Other men in the Mediterranean Fleet who were busy that night were the ships' carpenters—the "chippy chaps" —who had been ordered to make as many coffins as they could in time for the funeral arranged for the following day. Half a dozen bodies had been picked up immediately after the sinking, and the cruisers *Fearless, Barham,* and *Amphion* had remained behind until after dark, scouring the surface of the sea with their searchlights. At dawn the following morning the *Fearless* went out again and continued for forty-eight hours to patrol close to the coast, so close that she eventually went aground; and a riding party of Turkish cavalry rode up and down the beach for fourteen miles, bringing back much useless wreckage and reports of a curious thick stain over the water, which could only have been oil spreading out from the *Victoria*'s hull. The Turkish authorities were being very cooperative. The Sultan had at once sent a message of sympathy and offers of help, and, at his orders, a plot of land adjoining the city's wall was laid aside for consecration, the burial of the dead, and the erection of a memorial and a surrounding stone wall, for which his government would be happy to pay.

But no more corpses were found, either by the *Fearless* or by the Turkish cavalry, and the stacked-up coffins remained empty and only a corner of the emergency cemetery was eventually occupied by the bodies of Fleet Paymaster Valentine Rickord, a ship's steward, an interpreter, a cook, a sergeant of the Royal Marines, and A.B. Charles Tomkins.

At dawn on June 23, Markham issued orders for "a solemn funeral service to take place at 6:45 p.m. in memory of Vice-Admiral Sir George Tryon and the officers and men of Her Majesty's late ship *Victoria*, who perished in the appalling and ever to be deplored catastrophe." Frock coats, epaulettes, white trousers and shoes, and cocked hats were specified for officers, and swords were to be worn. Men were to attend in number 6 dress. At twenty minutes to sunset, a salute of seventeen minute guns was fired from the *Sans Pareil*, and the commander-in-chief's flag was hoisted at half-mast and struck as the sun went down. With the ships in two columns offshore, it was a moving moment in that wide bay when the bands struck up the admiral's salute, followed by a few bars from a funeral march, "and there were few present who could claim that their eyes were dry at the end of the service."

On Sunday, June 25, the wounded and those still suffering in some degree from the shock of their immersion—173 officers and men in all—were transferred to the battleship *Edgar* and the cruiser *Phaeton,* and early on the Monday morning these two ships steamed between the lines and out into the open sea. On the *Edgar* the wounded were made as comfortable as possible in beds, hammocks, and cots in the casemates, and Captain William Dyke-Acland had a cot hung in his own cabin for Commander Jellicoe, who was still in a weak condition. Four days later the *Edgar* and *Phaeton* arrived in Grand Harbour, Malta, and the bastions were packed black with curious onlookers, according to *The Times* correspondent, as the two ships steamed slowly to their moorings "amidst a solemn hush resembling that of a funeral." But none of the men were allowed ashore, and communication with the ships was prohibited, to the disgust of newspapermen and agency representatives ashore. Their readers would have, in the fullness of time, every detail of the sinking of the flagship and the experiences of her crew. But for the present the cause of the loss of the *Victoria* was *sub judice*.

The rest of the Mediterranean Fleet drifted back to Malta singly or in small groups, their flags at half-mast for their lost C.-in-C. and fellow seamen; and Valetta remained strangely subdued for some time. Only the *Camperdown* spoiled the air of solemnity and mourning. She was the last to return, her nose deep in the water and the collision mat still over her bows. But she did not appear downhearted by her injuries and trials, and "her band played lively airs on the quarter deck" as she swung into

Grand Harbour. "I remember thinking," Admiral Sir Charles Dundas recalls, "that on such a pathetic occasion it would have shown better taste if there had been less demonstration."

In the early hours of June 23, Flag Lieutenant Lord Gillford had wired his father, the Earl of Clanwilliam, "announcing his own safety but deploring the loss of Sir George Tryon." The old admiral thought that it must be either a hoax or that there had been an error in transmission. But the Admiralty had received the news an hour before, and already the telegraph room was choked with incoming and outgoing calls.

That evening, four thousand miles away at the Chicago Fair, Thomas Baker, Superintendent of the Transportation Building, wrote out a card in his own hand and propped it up against the magnificent scale model of the *Victoria,* "the most conspicuous naval exhibit there," according to the *New York Times.* "Total loss of the *Victoria,*" he headed it. "The *Victoria* foundered yesterday off Tripoli with a loss of 400 lives, the result of a collision with Her Majesty's Ship *Camperdown.*" Soon the crowds were so thick that the guards had to be called out to clear the aisles.

June 23, 1893, was a drizzly, dull day in London, and the Australians had a damp time beating Kent at Gravesend before going on to win the Ashes. In the Mall the stands were up for the wedding in four days' time of H.R.H. the Duke of York (later King George V) to Princess Victoria of Teck, and the flags hung limply along the procession route. Beerbohm and Mrs. Tree, with Miss Neilson, Miss Leclercq, Mr. Terry, and Mr. Kemble, were playing to

packed houses at the Haymarket in Mr. Oscar Wilde's
new play; Irving was playing opposite Ellen Terry as Portia
in *The Merchant of Venice* at the Lyceum; and George
Alexander was having a great success in Pinero's *The
Second Mrs. Tanqueray*. But the performances of the
Comédie Française at Drury Lane were being less well
received.

In the Commons, Gladstone and Chamberlain had been
fighting over the second Home Rule Bill. But when the
House assembled that morning, every member present had
already heard the news and anxiously awaited further word
from the Prime Minister. In the Lords, the Marquess of
Salisbury wished "to ask the noble Earl, the First Lord
of the Admiralty, whether he was in a position to give your
Lordship's House any information as to the news which
had been so widely spread throughout the country." But
as no more information than that contained in Markham's
first wire had so far been received, there was little either
Lord Spencer of Mr. Gladstone could add beyond expres-
sions of concern and sympathy for the bereaved. Similar
messages were already pouring in from all over the world,
from the Kaiser, now an Admiral of the Fleet in the Royal
Navy ("words cannot express our horror"); from President
Cleveland in the United States; from the President of
France, King Humbert of Italy, and all the other crowned
heads of Europe. Under the shock of such a catastrophe, the
perfidy of Albion could be forgotten for one day.

The Queen, who had been more closely associated with
the *Victoria* than with any other battleship in her Navy,
received the news at Windsor and at once dispatched a
message to Lord Spencer expressing her deepest grief:
"Her heart bleeds for the many homes which have been

plunged into mourning and deep affliction by this dreadful misfortune," she wrote, and she decided to cancel the state ball at Buckingham Palace arranged for that evening.

Lord Ancaster, George Tryon's brother-in-law, collected the Tryons' only son, Sub-Lieutenant George Clement Tryon of the 3rd Grenadier Guards, from Wellington Barracks, and together they went round to Eaton Place to break the news to Lady Tryon. After her first large reception of the season, she was still in bed at 11 a.m., "resting from the fatigue of that occasion when the sad truth was revealed to her." A stream of visitors followed Lady Tryon's nearest relatives: the Chamberlain of the Queen's Household; the Duchess of Teck; Lord Gillford's mother, Lady Clanwilliam; Captain Bourke's mother, the Dowager Countess of Mayo—"a ceaseless procession of the finest of the nobility," so many that she had a notice posted outside the house stating that "Lady Tryon, though in great grief, is very well." "The whole Navy weeps with you," Lord Charles Beresford wrote on the back of his card. "The State has lost its most brilliant seaman; the Navy its most generous and affectionate friend."

It was more than twenty-four hours before the first lists of drowned bluejackets and Marines were received, and by then the Admiralty was nearly in a state of siege, with strong forces of police holding back the anxious crowds of relatives and friends of the six hundred men of the *Victoria*'s lower decks. Trains had been bringing them in from all parts of the country during the day and through the following night, and several thousand were outside the gates by the morning of June 24, "their drawn faces and despondent attitudes showing the great strain they were undergoing," as the New York *Tribune*'s correspondent saw them.

Portsmouth and Chatham, the two naval towns from which many of the *Victoria*'s crew were drawn, had known sudden disaster before, but never on this scale; and at Portsmouth, according to one correspondent, "the greater part of the town was thrown into a panic" during that agonizing period before the long lists of dead were posted up.

At the other end of the social scale, in London's club-land, the meagre but appalling news which left so much for speculation dominated the luncheon conversation, and in the three service clubs, according to *The Times,* "the disaster cast a heavy gloom, and the anxious, sorrowful features of the naval men as they commented on the all-absorbing topic afforded striking testimony of the anguish of soul amongst them."

But over the succeeding days, as fuller details became available and every newspaper reader was able to follow the sequence of events that had led to the collision, the inevitable questions began to be asked. The public demanded to know who was to blame, and why the *Victoria* had sunk under such circumstances. On June 24 the *New York Times* correspondent in London had cabled his newspaper: "The tragedies of the ocean form a big and solemn part of England's history. It is only in the presence of such a sweeping calamity as that which gripped upon England's heartstrings yesterday that one came to realize how the sea still dominates the imagination of these islanders. . . . Later, when the personal aspects of the horror have worn off, there will be a fierce and bitter demand for a scape-goat."

To discover the scapegoat was not difficult. Publicly, and in the press, the many references to his name and the part he had played in the collision were accompanied by extravagant praise of his past service, his qualities as a leader, as the finest naval tactician in the world—and as an officer and a gentleman who had at least expunged his tragic blunder, and stood loyal to the best traditions of the service by going down in his ship. "The tragic blunder of a master-mind," was the phrase most often publicly resorted to at the time. But privately much harsher words were used among many in the Navy and some outside the service, among those who had clashed with his uncompromising will and self-assertiveness, suffered from his impatience, intolerance, and sharp tongue; among those who had seen him promoted over their heads and thrust his way to seniority; and even among those who had been offended by his blatant flouting of traditionalism. No man could reach senior rank in a peacetime service without risking un-popularity, and if Sir George Tryon was no more disliked than many commanders-in-chief had been before him, he had had his share of enemies. It might not be strictly within the code of fair play to throw the whole blame onto the one man unable to defend himself; but it was both natural and expedient. His was the only career that could not be shattered; and, in contrast with the reputation of so many living officers, that of one dead man must have seemed of trivial importance.

Only an American reporter would have dared to use the term "scapegoat" in these circumstances; there was no newspaper in England which cared to print such an un-happy word. But there was also no one in a position of authority or influence who doubted that Sir George Tryon, alone, had been responsible. The question "Who was to blame?" had been answered long before the official inquiry began to search below the surface.

8

Public opinion is justly dissatisfied and it is naturally asked whether and why our tremendous First Class ironclads are more dangerous to each other, and to their own crews and officers, than they might prove to be to a foreign enemy.

The Illustrated London News

"Why had the Victoria sunk?" was a question less easy to answer than "Who was to blame?" However, naval correspondents and naval theoreticians enthusiastically attempted to find the solution, and many reached some wild conclusions. But once the Admiralty had proved, at least to its own satisfaction, that the *Victoria*'s giant twin guns had not been responsible for her sudden end, a reasonable official explanation had to be provided for an anxious and angry public.

That she had sunk at all, in a flat calm, from a blow so far forward, was sufficient cause for concern about her construction. But the fact that she had turned over and capsized in ten minutes demanded investigation into the entire design policy of the Admiralty. The London *Standard* reflected the public's "most painful suspicion that the principles of shipbuilding which have prevailed in the Royal Navy for so many years may, after all, turn out to be unsound. . . . The most ignoble form of destruction which awaits a giant ship of war is that of being capsized," continued the writer. "To be sunk is paying a kind of homage to the ocean. To be capsized is, if we may be pardoned the phrase, almost to be made ridiculous. Our ships may be forgiven if they take a header, but to roll over topsy-turvy implies a grave fault somewhere."

The Admiralty succeeded in avoiding a general policy inquiry, but it was imperative that it should make public the technical reasons for the disaster. To be called on to explain how a first-class ironclad, costing £845,000 (over $4,000,000), could sink by collision with another warship travelling at a third of its maximum speed, in peacetime manœuvres on a calm sea and within a few miles of a friendly shore, was a challenging task. The cause could not be ascribed wholly to human error, and the first tentative official reaction was to suggest that the *Victoria*'s helm may have jammed and that the watertight doors had not been closed in time. It was also convenient to emphasize that the disaster did at least confirm the power of the ram, the efficacy of which as a weapon had recently been questioned; it had already been discarded by far-sighted French naval designers. "I sincerely trust that no one will suppose that, because the *Victoria* foundered after being rammed, her machinery was faulty," the ever conservative and reassuring Lord Charles Beresford told the press. "There was not a vessel afloat that could stand ramming like that. In my opinion the ram is the most fatal weapon in naval warfare —more fatal even than the torpedo." The influential Lord Brassey, editor of *Brassey's Naval Annual*, also considered that "the accident is likely to make officers in naval actions more disposed to use that weapon." The press confirmed this line. "Of all the weapons available for martime fighting, the ram is the most certain and the most deadly," wrote the *Sphere*'s naval correspondent. "A blow with the ram, even when delivered at half speed, requires only to get home to smash the stoutest ironclad ever built." Relatives and friends of those lost could not be expected to find much reassurance from this sort of argument, but at least it was faintly reassuring to the taxpayer.

In America, where, according to Brassey, "all that contributes to the offensive and defensive power of ships of war is studied with a deep interest," the news that the *Victoria* had been sunk by the power of the ram also provided comfort to her Navy Department. The ram had been a much fancied weapon for some years, in spite of the frustration of both the *Monitor*'s and the *Merrimac*'s attempts to finish off each other by ramming, in the first combat between ironclads. The United States Navy's main function was that of coast defence, and she possessed only three full-sized battleships. She relied chiefly on such fast, protected cruisers as the *Columbia,* a dozen of which, according to ex-Secretary Tracy[1] of the Navy Department, "would exterminate the commerce of any country." By comparison with those of the major European powers, the U.S. Navy was small and weak, but the authorities were prepared to experiment—with "pneumatic and dynamite guns," for example, and with "a submarine gun firing a torpedo shell." Only in its enthusiasm for the ram was the Navy Department retrogressive. It had even commissioned a vessel of 2000 tons, and with a speed of 17 knots, which was little more than a floating ram. Admiral Ammen's extraordinary ram *Kathadin* was designed to go into action at high speed, partially submerged and with only the armoured deck visible, cutting through the high, vulnerable

[1] Although unaware at the time of the story among the lower decks of the Mediterranean Fleet, he also supported the conviction that the *Victoria*'s oversize guns had caused her to capsize.

hulls of enemy ironclads before their guns could be brought
to bear on this most difficult target.

Thus the New York *Tribune,* for example, could describe the sinking as "a portentous reminder of the weakness of the vaunted modern navy," which is so "defenceless
under the impact of the ram." The New York *Advertiser*
went even further: "There is not an ironclad afloat today,"
it claimed, "that can stand the battering of raft sawlogs on
a fleet of Hudson River canal boats." To a nation that had
largely eschewed the heavy ironclad and shown its confidence in the ram, the manner of the *Victoria's* end gave a
certain satisfaction. And, in the circumstances, Charles
Cramp of Cramp and Son, shipbuilders of Philadelphia,
was prepared to be generous. "English-built rams," he said,
"are excellent."

The basic design of the *Victoria,* particularly with regard
to her watertight compartments and doors, was similar to
that of almost every battleship in the Royal Navy. If,
therefore, the official inquiry into her loss had shown that
there was some fundamental weakness in her construction,
the effect could have been disastrous. In simple terms,
Britannia would no longer have ruled the waves. If it were
once known that England's battleships were so susceptible
to damage that they could be sunk at the nudge of another
of their kind, her colonies all over the world might become
wide open to French, German, or Russian attack, and
not only in the Mediterranean would her influence be lost.
The implications behind the loss of one battleship and the
crippling of another in these circumstances were so far-
reaching and so threatening that a completely honest public
appraisal of the cause of the collision and the damage it had
caused was out of the question.

On the whole, those responsible for drawing up the report by the Assistant Controller and Director of Naval Construction, Mr. W. H. White, which was presented to both Houses of Parliament in November 1893, did their job well. The report was long, highly technical, and thoroughly reassuring. The suggestion was denied that if the side armour plating had not stopped short at the fore turret the damage would, at least, have been much reduced, and the *Victoria* would not have foundered, let alone capsized. Sir Edward Reed, the belligerent late secretary of the Institute of Naval Architects, had contended that the *Camperdown*'s ram would have been unable to penetrate the *Victoria* if she had been protected by armour at the bows. Under such a blow, the report stated, "the strongest armoured side ever constructed must have yielded." The failure to close the watertight doors in time was only a subsidiary cause of the ship's capsizing, critics claimed. There were a dozen battleships in the Navy "that were likely to capsize in a similar manner if they received like injury," said Reed. But the report also emphatically denied this, stating "that the interval of time which elapsed between the instant when orders were given to close watertight doors and hatchways, and the instant of actual collision (viz. about one minute) was necessarily inadequate for the complete fulfilment of that intention." The under-water protection of the *Victoria* (and, by implication, of every battleship in the fleet) was perfectly adequate. All that was required to prevent a similar catastrophe was a longer warning interval instead of the "insufficiently adequate" one on the *Victoria,* so that the doors could be closed properly. Automatic or self-closing doors were ruled out as "no new argument in favour of [their use] seems to arise out of the loss of the *Victoria*."

Nevertheless, it was not long before they were fitted to virtually every large warship in the Royal Navy. And finally, said the report, the capsizing did not "suggest any insufficiency of stability in the design of the vessel." But the *Victoria*'s sister ship, the *Sans Pareil,* was modified as a result of the collision, and the vast longitudinal bulkhead, the filling of which, critics claimed, had caused her to sink, was removed. She remained suspect and unpopular until she was sold for scrap for £26,000 in 1907.

The question "Why had the *Victoria* sunk?" was thus answered in November 1893, and neither Sir Edward Reed nor any other critic seemed prepared to argue the matter further. The answer to the question "Who was to blame?" had been settled unofficially, and with general satisfaction, within a week of the disaster. But there were certain service formalities to be concluded by the Admiralty. The question of the conduct not only of the commander-in-chief but also of all the officers and men of the *Victoria* now had to be investigated.

9

The English seemed to be very behind in tactics at the
time, a fact which was illustrated by the Tryon trial.
Grand Admiral von Tirpitz

On the morning of July 17, 1893, Her Majesty's Ship
Hibernia lay at anchor in Dockyard Creek, Malta Harbour,
spruce and correct in the detail of her turnout, her hull
gleaming black and buff, her decks stoned to a white almost
as pure as the white of her boats, her brasswork brilliant
in the intense midsummer sun. The *Hibernia,* an old
masted wooden three-decker with a long and worthy past,
had about her an air of dignified solemnity, like that of a
stout and long-retired admiral recalled to duty. She had
served with distinction since her launching in 1804 at the
blockade of Brest and the Tagus, had taken part in
numerous actions including the attack on the batteries at
Cassis in 1814, and had been the flagship of such venerated
admirals as Lord St. Vincent, Lord Gardner, and Sir Sidney
Smith. The *Hibernia* was now as obsolete as Nelson's
Victory at Portsmouth, no more than a floating hulk for the
accommodation of transient ships' companies, due soon to
be broken up; but her final period of service in the Royal
Navy was to be marked by an occasion which would be
remembered long after her battle honours had been forgotten. Across the length and breadth of her poop deck was
spread a white awning; and beneath it were arranged the

heavy mahogany chairs and tables for the most important naval court martial of the Queen's reign.

On July 3 the Secretary of the Admiralty had sent to Admiral Sir Michael Culme-Seymour, Bart., the new Commander-in-Chief Mediterranean, "a Warrant for a Court Martial, to be held under the 91st and 92nd sections of the Naval Defence Act, to enquire into the loss of H.M.S. *Victoria* and to try Captain the Honourable Maurice Archibald Bourke, and the survivors of that ship, for their conduct on this occasion."

Admiral Culme-Seymour, who was then on board H.M.S. *Hawke* at Portsmouth, had proceeded at once to Malta to take up his command, bringing with him the warrant. Culme-Seymour came from a distinguished naval family, which had produced three admirals in the past sixty years, and he had achieved his present rank and reputation by the competence, energy, and enthusiasm he had shown in almost all the minor naval campaigns since the Burmese War of 1852, from the bombing of Sevastopol to the capture of Canton. He managed his men and ships with wholly justified self-assurance and an efficiency which was now demonstrated by the completion of arrangements for the court martial at an unprecedented speed.

Culme-Seymour's secretary, Henry Hosking Rickard, was to officiate as deputy judge advocate; the prosecutor was to be the able and experienced Captain Alfred Leigh Winsloe of H.M.S. *Hawke;* and the members of the court, under the presidency of the C.-in-C., were made up of Vice-Admiral Tracey, the superintendent of Malta dockyard, who flew his flag on the *Hibernia,* and seven captains. After a good deal of difficulty and the exchanging of many interdepartmental memoranda, for the Admiralty was unprepared for such a prosaic contingency, a shorthand writer of sufficient speed to keep pace with the evidence at a long and detailed inquiry of this nature, one Arthur Herbert Moore, was obtained on lean from the Central News. His rate of pay, which the Admiralty considered excessive, was three guineas a day, plus eight pence per folio, and of course travel and living expenses.

On the stroke of nine o'clock, the court filed onto the poop deck, led by Sir Michael Culme-Seymour, a tall and drooping figure with a narrow, lugubrious face and a long hooked nose. Like five out of the eight members of his court, he had a full beard and side whiskers. It was already stiflingly hot beneath the awning, with no breath of wind to stir the paper laid out in a neat pile for each member on the polished table, with accompanying silver inkstands and quill pens. But, in accordance with naval etiquette, the officers wore their formal white uniforms, buttoned up to the neck, wore epaulettes and swords, and carried their heavy pith tropical helmets. Their silence repressed even the members of the press in their box, who, like orphanage children at a charity fête, were conscious that they were present only on sufferance. In point of law, the press could not be barred from a court martial, but there had been trouble more than once between the Admiralty and Fleet Street, most recently at the court martial of Vice-Admiral Fairfax for the stranding of H.M.S. *Howe,* when *The Times,* among other newspapers, had identified certain members of the court by name. It was Tryon who had led the attack against the press over the Fairfax court martial in a letter to the Secretary of the Admiralty. "I believe there is no legal objection," the admiral had written, "but there are grave naval objections to such a departure from naval practice." Over the court martial of Tryon's flag captain and the surviving crew of his flagship, however, the press behaved with punctilious correctness, governed, perhaps, more by regard for the tragic circumstances than by the late C.-in-C.'s injunction.

Shortly after nine o'clock the first of the boats carrying the prisoners began to come alongside the *Hibernia.* These were the 219 survivors among the petty officers and from the lower decks, and the 26 Royal Marines survivors. Eighteen more seamen were still recovering from their injuries in hospital, and three others were excused. In spite of the familiarity among them there was a certain feeling of unease among these old shipmates as they were rowed out and mustered on the main deck of the *Hibernia,* waiting to be called. During the past three and a half weeks they had covered every detail of their own and one another's experiences in the moments preceding, during, and after the disaster. There was left as a subject for conversation no single individual conjecture about the collision, and every speculation about the court martial had been exhausted. Everything had been discussed, in canteens and cafés, on and off duty by day, in their hammocks at night after turning in. In a life where friendships were often brief, even grief had begun to fade. Now there was probably not one among them who did not feel, at some moment and in some degree, at least a flutter of guilt that he had been, however indirectly, in part responsible for the disaster. Anxiety was present among them all, and anxiety was no stimulant to conversation among two hundred and fifty sailors, in clean bell-bottoms, freshly washed jerseys, and wide-brimmed straw hats, herded together on an unfamiliar main deck, awaiting court martial.

The officer prisoners had already arrived, in a steam picket boat, sternly uncommunicative on the short trip to the *Hibernia:* Captain Bourke, who would be bearing the greatest responsibility in the proceedings; Commander Jellicoe, pale from his fever; Lieutenants Heath and Leveson, whose technical evidence was to be so crucial; Staff Commander Hawkins-Smith, who had read his own obituary in several London newspapers; surgeons and engineering officers; a pathetic trio of youthful midshipmen out of eleven from the gunroom, although Midshipman Lumsden, who survives to this day, was expected to recover in hospital; and Major Arthur C. Smyth and Lieutenant Harry Farquharson of the Royal Marines. Absent, because as Admiral Tryon's staff they bore no technical responsibility for the handling of the ship, were three assistant paymasters, the late C.-in-C.'s secretary, and Flag Lieutenant Lord Gillford.

A few minutes after 9:30 the president of the court gave instructions for the prisoners to be brought in, and, preceded by armed naval guards in gaiters, the twenty-one surviving officers of H.M.S. *Victoria* filed in, followed in shuffling self-consciousness by the 245 petty officers, Marines, and bluejackets. These took station in a roped-off area behind their officers, who stood before a second table, this end of the "courtroom" being screened at the sides as well as by the big canvas awning overhead, to form a stage setting for the ten-day drama that lay ahead.

Last to be admitted was the audience, drawn from the officers of every ship of the Mediterranean Fleet, and the prosecutor, Captain Winsloe. It was past ten o'clock, the sun was approaching its zenith, and the temperature on the *Hibernia*'s packed poop deck was high into the nineties, when the seemingly interminable roll-call of the survivors was at last carried out. The tedious opening formalities were broken only by an objection by Captain Bourke to the inclusion on the court of four captains who "had been present at the occurrence to be inquired into." As one of these officers had commanded the *Camperdown*, the complaint certainly appeared to be justified, and was in fact allowed, four other officers of captain's rank taking their place. The consideration of this objection required the clearing of the entire courtroom, and it was nearly eleven o'clock before the swearing in of the court, the judge advocate, and the shorthand writer could take place.

Admiral Markham's letter to the Secretary of the Admiralty, written on the night after the disaster at Tripoli, was next produced and read out to the court by the deputy judge advocate. After detailing the orders and evolutions leading up to the moment when he had received from Tryon the order to turn, about which there could be no dispute, Markham had gone on:

"As the columns were only six cables apart, and therefore, not, in my opinion, within manœuvring distance to execute such an evolution as ordered by the signal in question, I directed my Flag-Lieutenant to keep the signal, which we were repeating, at the dip, as an indication that it was not understood. I then directed him to make a signal to the Commander-in-Chief to the following effect, by semaphore: 'Am I to understand that it is your wish for the columns to turn as indicated by the signal now flying?' but before my order could be carried out, the Commander-in-Chief semaphored to me to know 'what I was waiting for?' It then struck me that he wished me to turn 16 points as indicated by his signal, and that it was his intention to circle round the Second Division, leaving them on his port hand.

"Having the fullest confidence in the great ability of the Commander-in-Chief to manœuvre the Squadron without even the risk of a collision, I ordered the signal to be hoisted as an indication that it was understood.

"On the signal being hauled down, the helm of the *Camperdown* was put hard-a-port, at the same time that the helm of the *Victoria* was starboarded.

"I watched very carefully the helm indicating signals of the *Victoria*, as the two ships turned towards each other, and, seeing that the helm of the *Victoria* was still kept hard-a-starboard, I directed the Captain of the *Camperdown* to go full speed astern with his starboard screw, in order to decrease our circle of turning. Seeing that a collision was inevitable, I then gave orders to go full speed astern with both engines; but before the speed of the ship had been materially checked, the stem of the *Camperdown* struck the *Victoria* on her starboard bow. . . ."

This concise letter gave the court a clear picture of the situation on the *Camperdown*'s bridge as the fatal order was given. The signal from the flagship had apparently caused no more than a ripple of concern among the *Camperdown*'s senior officers while they wondered how the manœuvre could safely be carried out, until Tryon began to show his impatience, when the interpretation suddenly occurred to Markham. Of course the C.-in-C. did not intend the two columns to turn in on one another; he was going to take his column *round* the second division, to take the outer circle. That was it.

With Markham's letter were four enclosures, reports from the captain, two of the officers of the *Victoria*, and

Flag Lieutenant Lord Gillford. Of these, the report of Captain Maurice Bourke, the accused, was the most important, particularly as it made clear for the first time Tryon's plan for bringing the fleet into Tripoli harbour for anchoring. It was a characteristically ingenious plan, full of puzzles and surprises for his subordinates. The commander-in-chief, Bourke wrote, "said that he should form the Fleet in two divisions disposed to port, columns 6 cables apart, and when sufficiently past the line of bearing, namely the Tower of Lions, S. by E., which was the line we were going to turn up and anchor upon, he would invert the lines by turning the columns inwards 16 points, so that on reaching the line of bearing for turning up for anchoring, the Fleet should alter course together 8 points to port, bringing the Fleet in columns of divisions line abreast to port, columns disposed astern, steering S. by E., and anchoring on these bearings when Tares Island bore S. by W. . . ." (See the diagram on page 129.)

Finally, before the taking of evidence could begin, corrected and additional information was provided by Markham and his flag captain, Johnstone, in later letters to the Secretary of the Admiralty. "In reply to the signal made from the Commander-in-Chief to me by semaphore," wrote Markham nine days after the collision, " 'What are you waiting for?' I replied that I did not quite understand the signal." He also added that the *Victoria* had showed the *Camperdown*'s pendants "as an indication that an acknowledgement of the signal was immediately required."

Captain Johnstone revealed in his additional letter that he had made an unfortunate discovery. When the collision appeared inevitable and his admiral had given orders for full speed astern, both engines, he was convinced that,

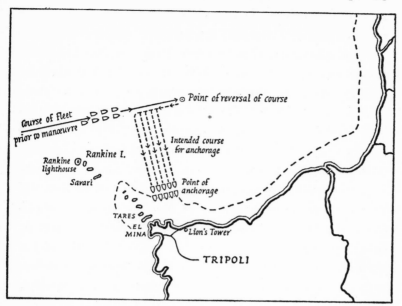

according to his custom, he saw the telegraph properly placed. But later, on reading the engine-room register, "I found to my astonishment that only three-quarters speed astern was recorded as having been given."

It was after midday, the sun was now beating down vertically, and there was hardly a breath of wind to disperse the odour of packed bodies under the white awning. Among the audience there had been many who had wished themselves ashore, but not after the reading of these two letters, which, unlike the earlier ones, had not previously been made public. Perhaps it was only natural that Markham should stress that he was under pressure to act on Tryon's order at once in a complex evolution within the restricted space of Tripoli Bay; and it was certainly fortunate that he had understood what had been expected of him in the nick of time. Perhaps, also, it could be understood, if not forgiven, that the order to reverse engines had not been correctly carried out under the tense circumstances of imminent collision. All the same, the picture of cool control on the bridge of the *Camperdown,* drawn from Markham's original dispatch, had already become somewhat clouded.

There were more surprises and revelations to come on that first tense morning. A few minutes after the reading of Captain Johnstone's letter, Joseph Newman, the chief constructor of Malta Dockyard, was called to answer a routine question about the condition of the *Victoria* when she had left after her refit. "Will you produce plans of H.M. Ships *Victoria* and *Camperdown?*" the president asked. A clerk from the constructor's office then stepped forward, holding in his arms a pile of documents showing section and plan drawings in every detail of every part of the flagship. "I produce the whole of the plans that I have in my possession," the chief constructor answered. And he would do better than this. "And a model of the *Victoria,*" he continued, "from the after boiler-room to the bows, with a section of the bow of the *Camperdown,* a skeleton section, in order that it may be placed into the *Victoria.*" The constructor had good cause to be pleased with himself as the two great models were placed, alongside the plans, in front of members of the court, dominating the table at which they sat so that officers sitting on opposite sides could not see one another. The work on the model had been beautifully carried out by the carpenters in the constructor's department, and they showed every important feature, such as compartments and watertight doors, without being cluttered with unnecessary detail.

"Captain the Honourable Maurice A. Bourke of Her Majesty's Ship *Victoria,*" the Clerk of the Court called out;

and Bourke arose and stepped forward, a tall, slim figure, flawlessly handsome, with a long, straight nose and wide-set brown eyes. His clean-shaven face, among so many bearded senior officers, made him appear even younger than he was. And yet, as he stood at attention in full tropical dress uniform, his white helmet under his arm, he looked confidently at ease and well able to look after himself. At a nod from the president, Bourke unsheathed his sword and placed it lengthways across the table, close to the models.

"Do the letters and their enclosures which have just been read to the Court furnish a true statement of the circumstances of the sinking of Her Majesty's late ship *Victoria?*" asked the president.

Bourke agreed that they did, and confirmed that he had no complaint against the conduct of any of his ship's officers and company.

The president than addressed himself to the packed mass of officers and men behind Bourke and asked them if they had any objections to the narrative or whether they had anything to lay to the charge of any other officer or man. There was a brief, tense pause followed by a murmur of negatives, led by the officers.

"All the surviving officers and men, except Captain Bourke, may now retire," Culme-Seymour announced. "I may just mention that technically the whole of the swords of the officers ought to be put on the table, but Captain Bourke's sword is put on as typical of the whole of them."

The men filed out once again, this time with a feeling of absolution. The skipper was to take the brunt—that was what he was paid for. And "Bourkey" knew how to look after himself.

Maurice Bourke then stood witness for the remainder of the day, until 4:30, with an hour and twenty minutes for luncheon. The long series of technical questions about the closing of bulkhead doors and the entry of water into the *Victoria*'s hull was broken once when, just before the luncheon adjournment, he stepped forward and man-œuvred the two ship models so that the skeleton *Camper-down* closed in on the *Victoria,* like some belligerent ghost ship intent on the destruction of its more tangible compan-ion, and drove itself against her hull plates. As the two flag-ships met, Bourke's voice, distinctively clear in the silence of the court, only emphasized the macabre unreality of this re-enactment of the scene. "The bow of the *Camperdown* was seen by the men in the fore mess deck, but not, ap-parently, by the men in the stokers' mess deck," he said, pointing out their position; and then a moment later: "The Admiral on the chart house hailed the *Camperdown* to go astern." And the two incidents, the one ridiculous and almost bizarre, the other so futile under the circumstances, seemed to be lent added pathos by the flat, cultivated tone in which they were recounted. "The only damage that I saw was the damage done to the upper deck, which was cut into, and all the deck ploughed into, broken up, and set back towards amidships. . . ."

It seemed at that moment that it might be impossible to ruffle this coolly self-confident young officer. But in fact his evidence on that opening day of his trial both began and ended on an emotional note which revealed a certain vulnerability in his character. After asking the president if he could add something to his earlier written statement, he described the moment when he had been alone with Tryon on the sternwalk of the *Victoria.* "I must beg the Court to excuse me saying anything about what I said to the Admiral under the circumstances," he said emphatically.

"Do you state that on the ground that you do not wish to incriminate yourself?" the president asked.

"No, sir. I do not wish to have anything said about it at all. The subject was discussed between the Admiral and myself. I can go as far as that. The question is a very serious one for me. Whatever I said, he is gone, and cannot qualify my statement. I am on my oath, but under the circumstances, I would rather not say anything at all about it."

Three times more Culme-Seymour pressed Bourke without success. "The point is, you are asked a question as to what passed," he told him firmly, now showing irritation, "and there is no doubt by the law you can only refuse to answer on the plea that it tends to incriminate yourself."

There was a moment's silence in the court, and then Bourke said in a low voice, "I reminded the Admiral that our circle was eight hundred yards. He said the columns were to remain at six cables. I then went on deck."

So Tryon had been reminded again, this time by his own captain, that the distance between the two flagships was 1200 yards and that the diameter of the *Victoria*'s circle alone was 800 yards. The *Camperdown*'s turning circle, as Bourke stated a few minutes later, was "practically the same," serving to confirm all expert opinion that the C.-in-C. had ordered the evolution to be carried out in the full knowledge of its inevitably disastrous consequences. It appeared that Bourke had done everything, within the limits of naval discipline, to dissuade him. And the sympathy of all those present was so strongly on the side of the unfortunate captain that it is unlikely that a single person questioned at the time Bourke's roundabout and apparently reluctant method of stating this strong piece of evidence in his own favour, and against that of "my chief and my kindest friend." He had volunteered the information that he had been alone with Tryon on the sternwalk. No one had prompted him. And yet he must have known that, under the rules of courts martial, he would be obliged to tell what passed between them. If he really did "not wish to have anything said about it at all," why, then, had he opened up the subject?

If there was a slight element of the unseemly in this early passage, there was no question of the sincerity of Bourke's answer to one of the president's last questions of the day. "Can you account for the great number of men drowned?" he was asked.

The prisoner was by then clearly very tired. He had been standing or sitting at the table reserved for the accused and witnesses, in the close, burning heat, for the best part of a day, under extreme emotional stress. If his words occasionally tumbled out incoherently he could be forgiven. "I think that, unfortunately, amongst the stokers and the Marines there was a very large proportion who could not swim," he began uncertainly and in a voice that occasionally broke into a half-sob. "Except those, unfortunately, in the boiler room and engine room, I am of the opinion that every single soul in the ship was on deck, fallen in on the port side of the upper deck. As I say, I do not think anyone in the ship really appreciated—I certainly did not—that at the heel we were at, the ship was going to turn over at that moment. . . . I do not suppose there will be another opportunity of saying it, but I think it shows the wonderful command that everybody had over himself, that not one single man fell out to go to the ship's side. Just at the last, Lieutenant Heath gave the order 'Jump,' and he is, I think, the only officer or the only person who gave any order. Nobody, I think, can say that the Commander-in-Chief gave any order. . . .

"The ship sank in, I think it was, from seventy-five to eighty fathoms; the ship is roughly sixty fathoms long, and I think what must have happened was, that when she struck the bottom, going headfirst down, at that moment the boilers must have gone, and the whole thing gone to pieces, and up came this enormous swirl of water carrying with it spars and wreckage and things, and undoubtedly a great many men must have been struck by spars and things, because of the number even now who are in hospital with broken ribs."

The consequences of that fatal swirl, that "tremendous surge of water," provided a fitting and sombre curtain to the day's evidence. A gunner in the water, Bourke said, "declares that he was amongst crowds of men, he describes it as crowds of men—the water was perfectly thick with them—and he went down in consequence of this swirl, and when he came up he saw hardly any men." It had destroyed all but the strongest swimmers. "They were nearly all gone," Bourke ended, his head lowered.

It was not only the members of the press who were aware that the climax of the court martial would be provided by Rear Admiral Hastings Markham and his flag captain, Johnstone. Their appearance on the *Hibernia* and their evidence was awaited eagerly by every officer and man at Malta. They were expected to be called on the second day, after Captain Bourke had concluded his evidence, and this seemed to be confirmed when the *Nile,* on which Markham now flew his flag, steamed into Malta Harbour just as the court was assembling, and headed towards the *Hibernia.* The two men appeared as if determined to make a splendid entrance. The *Nile* was the finest and most modern battleship in the Mediterranean, and everyone turned to watch her great black hull steaming slowly across the smooth water. "Her band was playing," wrote Reuter's correspondent, "and her decks were alive with men, presenting a gallant spectacle in the glorious morning sunshine, and contrasting strangely with the sombre character of the day's proceedings." Behind the *Nile,* the *Victoria*'s identical sister ship heaved into sight like a ghostly conscience and anchored near the harbour entrance. The final touch of appropriate majesty to the scene was provided when Markham left his flagship and approached the *Hibernia* in his barge. The formal thirteen-gun salute was fired in his honour, and he made his way up the ladder and disappeared into Admiral Tracey's cabin to confer with Culme-Seymour. But it was soon evident that Markham's hour had not, after all, yet come. He left five minutes later, and the court assembled to hear Bourke's continued evidence.

It was to be another harrowing day for Tryon's flag captain. Culme-Seymour was still unsatisfied that the court had been told of everything that Bourke and Tryon had said to each other on the *Victoria*'s sternwalk. "State to the Court," he was told, "all that took place between you. . . ."

"The interview I am referring to did not last more than a minute after the Flag-Lieutenant had left the sternwalk," Bourke said. "To the best of my belief, the Commander-in-

Chief said to me, rather shortly, something to the effect that 'That's all right. Leave it at six cables,' and then I left the cabin. That was all that passed between us."

Again Culme-Seymour probed him on this vital point, without further result, and the questioning went on to other matters. "When the signal was hauled down, had you any clear idea in your own mind as to what should be done to avoid the collision?" "Will you explain to the Court why the order to close watertight doors was not given before?" "Will you state to the Court how the signal for six cables came to be flying after the Commander-in-Chief had practically assented to eight cables?"

Sitting erect in the chair now provided for him at the lower corner of the table, Bourke creditably withstood the barrage from the president and other members of the court. Then came the inevitable question. "Did it not strike you that the Admiral, by some mischance, was confusing the distance of the radius of the circle, namely two cables, with the diameter of the circle which was four cables, when he ordered the divisions to be six cables apart?"

This was what the press representatives had been waiting for. This theory was the popular one, the one that had been expressed with positive self-assurance by every newspaper's naval correspondent and repeated in every pub and club in Britain. This was "the tragic blunder of a master mind." It was so simple and so plausible. But there was no pat answer from Bourke. "I can hardly say what struck me," he replied, again showing signs of the emotional strain under which he was suffering. "It could not have struck me in that light, because I think I should have said so; but at this distance of time it seems to me that I had some idea in my head that the Commander-in-Chief had some way out of it. My impression was that something was going to happen. I had confidence in the Commander-in-Chief, and nobody ever questioned him. I never questioned him."

How difficult it was to discover the truth! A few minutes earlier Bourke had been asked when it had first occurred to him that there was the danger of collision. His reply seems to crystallize the problem of finding the truth in any inquiry, into any sudden disaster. "I should like to state to the Court," he said, "that so much has passed since the accident, so much has been said, and so much have I thought about the thing, that it is very difficult for me to say, exactly, what my impressions were at the time. There is no doubt that in an accident of this sort, one can almost make oneself believe one's impressions were anything."

One other subject that was bound to be raised came up that morning, that old thorny subject of T.A. manœuvring. "Who conned the *Victoria* when manœuvres were being carried out?" Bourke was asked.

"When not exercising with T.A., the Commander-in-Chief remained aft," Bourke said. "I do not think I remember a single case of his being forward at ordinary manœuvres." But he had come forward to supervise this particular evolution. This, then, as the court at once suggested, "was quite an exceptional case." Nothing had been said to indicate that T.A. had been in effect at the time of the collision, and yet the C.-in-C. had been forward, a position he occupied only when manœuvring under T.A. The question of T.A. was to be raised again later, but for the present it was to be passed by. It was an uncomfortable subject.

It was 11:30 and the temperature in the courtroom was

even higher than on the first day. As Captain Bourke withdrew, Culme-Seymour told the officers present that, in view of the heat, coats could be taken off. The members of the court were assisted out of theirs, and the garments were placed neatly over the backs of their chairs, the example being followed by the officer prisoners, the members of the audience and the press representatives.

Lord Gillford was then called and sworn in, and was invited to take a seat at the table beside Bourke.

The prosecutor took over, first inviting Gillford to add to his earlier statement. He had little that was new to tell and contented himself with a detailed account of what he had personally done, what he had seen and what he had heard, much of it again of a technical nature. But shortly before the adjournment for luncheon, the whole issue, the entire *raison d'être* of the court martial, appeared for one moment to have been resolved.

"Did you hear the Admiral at any time after the collision pass any remark as to whom, if anyone, he blamed for having caused it, or suggest any reason for its cause?"

"Yes," Lord Gillford replied, asking, when pressed, if he was bound to repeat what he had heard. At this point Culme-Seymour intervened, as he had before, when Bourke had shown reluctance to answer. "You are bound to answer every question that is asked you unless it tends to incriminate yourself," he repeated.

And, like Bourke, Lord Gillford paused before replying in a low voice: "The Admiral said 'It was all my fault.' "

A dozen questions followed in quick succession, each of trivial importance after this startling revelation. And then inevitably the court returned to this situation, this picture of the admiral standing above the bridge of his own doomed flagship, confessing that its fate, and the fate of his own men, had been entirely his own doing.

"Did he say it to you or was it a general expression?"

"I believe no one heard that expression except myself," Lord Gillford said.

"He addressed you, did he?"

"I believe so—he was not looking directly at me, but was standing alongside me, and immediately afterwards sent me below."

After the youthful Lord Gillford and the young middle-aged flag captain, Staff Commander Thomas Hawkins-Smith appeared elderly. Grey-haired and grey-bearded, he looked like a failed fading schoolmaster up before the Head. Speaking slowly and with less self-assurance than either Gillford or Bourke, he too enlarged on his written statement, and this was followed by the usual technical questions about turning circles, reversing of the screws and the helm, none of which produced any replies of great significance.

Who remained on the bridge after the collision? Hawkins-Smith was asked by the prosecutor, and he told the court that only Lord Gillford and he had been left with Tryon. "There was no conversation, but he made use of an expression," he volunteered. "He said: 'It is entirely my doing, entirely my fault.'"

Any further doubts about the final responsibility for the collision must surely now be dispelled on this further confirmation of Tryon's complete acceptance of the blame. And yet, as was to happen time and again throughout the court martial, the apparent paralysis of initiative which seized every officer in the two flagships who might have prevented disaster was revealed in Hawkins-Smith's further answers. On being asked if he had said anything to Tryon about the closeness of the columns after the admiral had come up onto the bridge, he replied simply, "No, I was never asked for my advice . . . I said nothing at all"; and this despite his own vehement protests to Tryon's flag lieutenant on learning that the distance was to be six cables. When asked if he had suggested that the use of the screws might prevent a collision, Hawkins-Smith answered with a flat negative. "Did it occur to you to express an opinion on the subject to anybody?" "No," Hawkins-Smith replied.

There was also an important inconsistency in Hawkins-Smith's evidence which passed, like so many others at this court martial, without comment. He had, he reported, tried to persuade Tryon to make the distance between the columns eight cables; and yet later in the afternoon, when asked, "Do you consider eight cables was a sufficient distance for the divisions to be apart?" he had replied, "No."

Staff Commander Hawkins-Smith did, however, succeed in clearing up one serious misconception. The point on which Tryon had been attacked by some naval authorities, by the press, and by public opinion in general, and one which had caused much anger among relatives of the drowned men, was his action in ordering back to their ships the boats launched before the capsizing of the *Victoria* to pick up any survivors. To continue to drive his sinking ship towards the shore, even refusing all offers of aid, seemed to many to prove the extreme degree of the admiral's conceit. But Hawkins-Smith had told the admiral "that she ought to keep afloat for some time," and, as every other witness from the *Victoria* testified, no one thought that the ship was near her end until the moment before she cap-

sized. He also made clear that this order of Tryon's was
not a gesture of false confidence for, as the C.-in-C. ordered
the *Victoria* to be steered towards the Tripoli coast in the
hope of beaching her, he had ordered an open signal to be
made "to form on each corner" with boats slung out or in
tow, so that they would not be left behind, although the
flagship went down before there was time to hoist it.

The day closed on a mainly technical note, with the
cross-examination by the prosecutor of Lieutenants Herbert Heath and Charles Collins, the officer of the watch,
both of whom had struggled without success to get the
collision mat over the huge hole caused by the *Camperdown*'s ram and prow. But neither these officers nor Markham nor any other officer of the *Camperdown* and *Victoria*
was questioned at any time during the court-martial proceedings on the apparent urgent importance attached to
separating the two flagships. It does not seem to have
occurred to anyone, then or subsequently, in reference to
the collision, that if the ships had been left locked together,
at least until all the watertight doors had been closed, the
flooding of the *Camperdown* might have been much reduced, and the *Victoria* even saved from capsizing.

The court martial's most important witness was called
at last when the court reassembled on the third morning,
a morning that was as clear and fine and brilliantly hot as
every other day of the trial. Rear Admiral Markham's
position was not an easy one, for it was clearly evident to
everyone that he was, if not yet a prisoner, as much a
defendant as Bourke and every other officer and man of
the *Victoria*, although he had none of the privileges of a
defendant. Later, this anomaly was recognized officially, and

he was permitted to suggest questions that the court might ask of witnesses and to sit alongside witnesses at the second table.

As on the previous morning, Markham was received on board the *Hibernia* with a salute of thirteen guns, and was at once sworn in and invited to sit down next to Bourke. He looked dour and apprehensive, and conscious as always of his rank, as his examination by the prosecutor began.

Asked to state what passed through his mind when the signal to turn was hoisted on the *Victoria*, Markham expanded his original statement and repeated some conversation which had occurred during those anxious moments before the helm of his flagship was put over. "It is impossible as it is an impractical manœuvre," had been his response when the meaning of the signal had been explained to him by his flag lieutenant. He had ordered the signal to be kept at the dip as an indication that he did not understand it, while he made his way to the forebridge. On the way he had met his flag captain and had said to him: "It's all right. Don't do anything. I have not answered the signal." Markham had then made his way back to the after bridge and come forward with his flag lieutenant for a second time, when a discussion was held between the three officers on the bridge. "He will invert the line," was the opinion of one of Markham's officers when they had been considering earlier how the squadron could be got onto its anchorage bearings. But to this, Markham had, he said, demurred. "I am quite sure he will not carry out such a very dull and prosaic manœuvre," he had told his flag captain. And Markham had been proved right. This was not only unorthodox but incomprehensible—until suddenly the correct interpretation "flashed across my mind" that he was to put his helm down and turn 16 points to starboard, "and that the *Victoria* would ease her helm down and circle round outside of my division." This, it had seemed to Markham, was "the only way to get our ships properly on our anchorage bearings," and his flag captain and flag lieutenant had agreed.

On being asked by the prosecutor what the diameter of the *Camperdown*'s turning circle was at nine knots, Markham said he thought it was about six hundred and sixty yards, though he was not sure. "With the columns at six cables apart," Captain Winsloe then asked, "suppose the ships to turn towards each other with full helm, did the absolute certainty of a collision occur to you?"

"Most certainly."

"When the Commander-in-Chief semaphored 'What are you waiting for?' will you read from the signal log your reply?"

" 'Three-thirty-two p.m. From *Camperdown* to Flag— Did not quite understand the signal.' "

From later evidence, given on that day by Markham's flag lieutenant, it was made clear that this signal was sent after the *Camperdown*'s helm was put over and the evolution had commenced, although no reference to this discrepancy was made by the prosecutor at this stage. Instead he asked if Markham had "been aware, on the morning of 22nd June, of a memorandum, which had previously been issued by Sir George Tryon, bearing on the subject of discretion in obeying orders." Markham confirmed that he had, and Captain Winsloe then asked the deputy judge advocate to read out to the court this memorandum:

Victoria at Malta

"It may frequently happen that an order may be given to an officer which, from circumstances not known to the person who gave it at the time he issued it, would be impossible to execute, or the difficulty or risk of the execution of it would be so great as to amount to a moral impossibility."
—*Duke of Wellington's G.O. November 11, 1803.*

1. While an order should be implicitly obeyed, still circumstances may change and conditions may widely vary from those known or even from those that presented themselves at the time orders were issued. In such cases the officer receiving orders, guided by the object that he knows his chief had in view, must act on his own responsibility.

2. (a) Orders directing the movements of ships, either collectively or singly, are invariably accompanied, as a matter of course, with the paramount understood condition, with due regard to the safety of Her Majesty's ships.

(b) When the literal obedience to any order, however given, would entail a collision with a friend, or endanger a ship by running on shore, or in any other way, paramount orders direct that the danger is to be avoided, while the object of the order should be attained if possible.

3. An Admiral lending a fleet relies with confidence that, while the "order" of the fleet is maintained, each ship will be handled and piloted with all the care and attention that is exercised in the guidance of the leading ship. He relies that this will be the case more especially when a fleet is approaching land or a harbour. . . .

4. Risks that are not only justifiable, but are demanded during war, are not justifiable during peace.

G. Tryon. Vice-Admiral and Commander-in-Chief.

Was it merely ironically coincidental that Tryon had issued to his subordinates this reminder of their responsibilities just before the fleet had sailed under his command for the last time? Or perhaps it had been Tryon's intention deliberately to challenge their initiative and attention to the safety of their ships? Certainly the reading of this memorandum caused the greatest impact of any incident in the court martial, and led to the widest comment in the newspapers the following day.

"When the turning signal was flying, did you remember the provision in Article 2, paragraphs (a) and (b) of that memorandum?" Winsloe demanded of Markham.

"I do not know that those Articles were actually running in my head, but the safety of my ship and division certainly was," Markham replied.

"How do you account for your action in the manœuvre, bearing in mind the directions contained in that Article?"

Markham began to show his impatience. "Because, as I said before, I thought the First Division were going to wheel round me, which would have been a manœuvre of perfect safety, and a feasible one." And, pressed to suggest how he came to that conclusion, "Because it was the only safe interpretation of the signal. The other was an absolute impossibility."

Further sharp questioning by Winsloe revealed that Markham had watched very closely the helm signals of the *Victoria,* which would have revealed, moment by moment, the sharpness of her turn; that when the two flagships were in a direct line, bow to bow, with each other, they were two cables apart; and that at that point "it was impossible for the *Camperdown* to prevent a collision unless she went against the rule of the road." Markham also considered that the fact that the *Camperdown*'s engines were going only three-quarters astern instead of full astern as ordered had made little difference to the impact between the two vessels, although "the blow might have been a

little lighter." While the two ships had been locked together, had there been any conversation between them?
Tryon had come over to the starboard side of the bridge,
Markham answered, "and said something to me. I walked
over to the port side of our bridge, to be close to him and
hear what he said, but could not do so on account of the
noise that was made by our boat hoist."

Winsloe then switched his line of cross-examination,
easing the pressure on Markham by concentrating on com-
paratively straightforward technical questions and matters
of simple observation after the collision. At this point
Culme-Seymour intervened to ask Markham if he was
aware of a recent amendment in the General Signal Book
which read: "Although it is the duty of every Ship to preserve as correctly as possible the Station assigned to her,
this duty is not to be held as freeing the Captain of the
responsibility of taking such steps as may be necessary to
avoid any danger to which she is exposed, when immediate
action is imperative, and time or circumstances do not
admit of the Admiral's permission being obtained." No, he
was not aware of this, Markham confirmed.

And Winsloe at once returned to the attack. He still
wanted to know why the rear admiral had presumed that
Tryon would circle round him. Because anything else was
impossible, Markham repeated, and because every ship in
the fleet had already answered the flagship "and therefore I
expected that the captains had understood the signal in the
same way that I did." Had his decision perhaps been rather
hurried? suggested Winsloe. And then the calm resolution
on the forebridge of Markham's flagship, suggested by the
formal written statement, was wholly contradicted by the
rear admiral's confession.

"I knew that the squadron was proceeding towards the land at a speed of about nine knots, and that we had already passed the bearings on which I thought the Commander-in-Chief was going to anchor, and that there was no time for me to question the Commander-in-Chief as to his intentions. Nor did I think it was right for me to do so," Markham concluded, "after having put the interpretation which I did upon his signal."

But there can be only one interpretation of any signal, according to the signal book, Winsloe persisted. "Will you explain to the Court how you interpreted it differently from the way in which it was carried out?"

"I did not even know that the signal was in the signal book," Markham confessed. "I interpreted what I considered the safe and only way of carrying it out; and I must say that I had the utmost confidence in my leader."

The sort of situation that had apparently created this confidence, a confidence which Markham frequently emphasized, was described by him later that morning. "We used to carry out many evolutions in the Mediterranean Squadron of which at the time, I must acknowledge, I hardly knew what was the object, and they were only afterwards fully explained to me by the Commander-in-Chief in his cabin. It has not infrequently occurred to me that when I have gone on board after anchoring the squadron, the Commander-in-Chief has said: Do you know why I did so and so? and I have said No, sir, why? and then it has been explained to me, and I had some sort of idea of that in my head at the time, when I ordered the signal to be answered. I thought he was going to wheel round me and come up somewhere on the other side and re-form his squadron."

Five minutes later, with the luncheon adjournment now imminent, Winsloe switched back again to the moment when the two flagships were bows on. "Do you think," he asked, "if you had shifted your helm to hard-a-starboard and the *Victoria*'s helm had remained as it was, you would have gone clear?"

"No; and I should have been utterly wrong in doing it." In other words, it would have been wrong for the *Camperdown* to swerve to the left in an effort to avoid the *Victoria* because, as Markham had explained earlier, it would have been against the rule of the road.

"Are you aware that the rule of the road does not apply in manœuvres?" Winsloe asked blandly.

"Yes."

"I think in a former question that you referred to the rule of the road?"

"I did, in one of my former answers," Markham confessed.

Rear Admiral Markham withdrew. The ordeal was over for the present. That evening he wrote in his diary: "I was the first witness to be examined today, and am by no means happy at the result of the examination."

Early in the afternoon on the third day, Markham's flag captain, Charles Johnstone, was called and was at once attacked by Winsloe with a series of questions which made clear that, like his admiral, he had been completely confused by the "mistaken signal" to turn, even after he had called for the signal book and looked it up. Only its interpretation by Markham, when he came forward, fully satisfied him. "Oh yes, the Admiral intends to circle round us," Markham had told him, and Johnstone fully agreed with that conclusion. It was not until an hour later, for Winsloe spaced his questions as cleverly as an experienced barrister, that Johnstone contradicted himself.

"Were you convinced at the time you put your helm over that it was the intention of the Commander-in-Chief to circle round the division?"

"No, I was not convinced," Johnstone replied.

Again and again during that afternoon Johnstone prevaricated and equivocated. He could not explain how the engines were running only three-quarters astern when full astern had been given in an attempt to slow the speed of the ship. He would not acknowledge that either he or Markham had endangered their ship by interpreting the signal as they had, for "had any other movement been made, . . . the Commander-in-Chief's intentions must have been entirely frustrated, and perhaps great danger of collision incurred." Although "the die was cast" when the two ships put over their helms, Johnstone revealed that only 28 degrees of helm had been given instead of the full 34 degrees. But when it was later suggested to him that if full helm had been given and starboard screw reversed a collision might have been avoided, he agreed; adding, however, that this would have "almost certainly" resulted in a collision with the *Camperdown*'s next astern, a view which he modified when pressed by suggesting that such an occurrence might not have happened "exactly in those words," although confusion would certainly have prevailed. He also thought, contrary to the opinion of his rear admiral, that the rule of the road applied on manœuvres unless expressly stated to the contrary.

Captain Johnstone's evidence, which ran over into the fourth day of the court martial, left the court and the

audience in an uncertain state of mind about the true
sequence of events, and even the authenticity of some of
them, which had occurred on board the *Camperdown* during those last crucial minutes. As to the sequence of impressions and thoughts that had passed through the minds of
the rear admiral and his flag captain, these, too, seemed
equally unclarified. There was complete agreement between them only on the conversations that had occurred,
and it was soon revealed their accounts of these were either
inaccurate or incomplete.

After Johnstone had withdrawn on the fourth day, the
Camperdown's officer of the watch gave evidence that he
heard Markham still expressing bewilderment about the
meaning of the signal at a time when he had testified that
he had understood Tryon's intentions. "I heard him say to
the Captain that he thought that they were probably going
to do it by divisions one at a time by hauling down one
signal at a time," Acting Lieutenant Alexander Hamilton
stated. And the fact that Markham was still confused when
he came forward from the after bridge for the second time
was confirmed by the *Camperdown*'s navigating officer,
Lieutenant Francis Barr:

Question 624. PROSECUTOR: Will you state what you heard?—
Admiral Markham came forward to the forebridge, while
Captain Johnstone was looking out the signal, and he said:
"We cannot do it. It is impossible. We are not at the manœu-
vring distance." Then he said to the Flag-Lieutenant, I believe:
"Do not hoist that signal," and then he went aft again.

625. Before the repetition signal was hoisted close up, did
you hear anything else?—Yes.

626. Will you state it?—Admiral Markham came forward
again and said: "They mean it, Captain Johnstone, we shall
have to do it. They have asked me what I am waiting for."

Later, on the prosecutor's returning to the conversation on the forebridge when Markham came forward for the second time, Lieutenant Barr testified: "Shortly before the helm was ordered over, he [Markham] remarked to me: 'We cannot do this, can we?' and I said: 'No, it is not possible.' He then remarked, partly to me and partly to Captain Johnstone, who was standing by: 'He must be going to circle round us, passing us on the port hand.' Then he said: 'What is the rule, Johnstone, port side to port side?' Captain Johnstone said: 'I believe so' or words to that effect."

From this it appeared that Markham's final interpretation of the signal came to him, not only less emphatically than he had suggested, but also a good deal later. It also seemed curious that he should have to refer to a junior officer for confirmation of the impracticability of the manœuvre, and that neither he nor his captain was certain of the rule of the road—which in any case did not apply under the circumstances.

"My position was a peculiarly painful one," ran an entry in Markham's diary, "for it was difficult for me to justify the course I took without, in a measure, implying culpability to Sir George Tryon." To an unprejudiced judgement he had, at the end of the fourth day, hardly succeeded on either count.

Before the fifth day of the hearing it had become apparent to the audience and the press that the nature and direction of the court martial had been completely altered. If no verdict had yet been passed on Captain Bourke and the officers and crew of the *Victoria*, it had already been

established that they were innocent of any neglect of duty
or of risking their ship. Whatever occurred on the flagship
that afternoon that might have led to the disaster was not
their responsibility. On the other hand, the evidence of
Markham and his flag captain and his flag lieutenant, was
clearly so unsatisfactory and had revealed so many con-
tradictions and inconsistencies, as well as a situation
amounting almost to pandemonium on the bridge of the
Camperdown, that the question of mishandling and neglect
of duties on that ship had to be further investigated. Markham had no illusions about his position. The sword lying
across the table might belong to Captain Bourke, but it was
his own future that was at stake. By taking advantage of
the unusual privileges afforded to him, he prepared to fight
back from the weak tactical position into which the unexpected turn of events had forced him.

Markham had heard, he said, from "information that has
been given to me unsolicited," that other captains in the
squadron had interpreted the signal as he had. He therefore
asked Culme-Seymour, in justice to himself, if he might
call three of the captains to give evidence on this. That
was perfectly in order, he was told. But, Culme-Seymour
warned, "You are aware of course that the Court will
probably call other captains whom you have not named as
to the same point?" If Markham had not, perhaps, considered this consequence of his request, there was nothing
he could do now but accept it.

Apart from some technical information, supplied mainly
by the engineering staffs of the two flagships, the rest of the
proceedings was then occupied with the evidence of eight
of the Mediterranean Fleet's captains, all of whom had

been faced with the interpretation of Tryon's unusual and apparently dangerous signal, even if their responsibility had been less onerous than Markham's.

Two of the three captains Markham had wished to call agreed completely with him. Dyke-Acland of the *Edgar*, the fourth ship in Markham's division, considered the manœuvre an impossible and dangerous one when he first understood its meaning; but, like Markham, "it then flashed across my mind that there was no way of carrying out that signal unless one division circled round the other." Brackenbury, who had been astern of the *Camperdown*, also agreed, and "had no doubt that the Admiral would go outside." But Captain Vandermeulen of the *Inflexible* failed to support Markham when he was called later. He had interpreted the signal as a turn inwards and nothing else, however dangerous it might be; and he also thought "that the signal ought not to have been answered without a question being asked." Custance of the *Phaeton* and Jenkins of the *Collingwood* were of the same mind; while Wilson of the *Sans Pareil*, a future admiral of the fleet, also concurred, although he "knew an accident would take place if they turned inwards, but, considering the confidence I had in my leaders, I felt sure that they had made some arrangements which would prevent it." Captain Arthur William Moore of the *Dreadnought* also disagreed with Markham's interpretation. "I thought we were about to see something unusual in the way of an evolution. . . . What flashed across my mind was this, We are going to see something interesting; how are they going to do it? I think I made the remark, 'How on earth shall we do this?' "

One of the last to be called was Gerard Noel of the *Nile*, the most experienced sailor present, whose ship had been

next astern of the *Victoria*. When he too gave evidence that
he expected that the two flagships would turn inwards,
taking "such steps as to turn inside the three cables, which
was the limit of their turning clear of each other," Markham must have regretted appealing to the court for permission to call for the supporting evidence of Tryon's subordinates.

"Did it occur to you that it was a dangerous manœuvre?"
Winsloe asked Noel.

"I have been nearly two years on the station with the
Nile," he replied. "I have entered port or anchorage over
fifty times in company with the late Commander-in-Chief.
. . . On no occasion can I remember that a signal has been
made which I did not fully understand, and which was not
a perfectly safe one. Whilst manœuvring at sea we were
accustomed to see signals made which were unexpected,
but never one that was dangerous. This has caused on my
part a most perfect confidence in the admirable manner in
which the fleet was invariably conducted." Noel was a tall,
striking figure, and everyone present responded to his
fluent evidence that was not only delivered with deep conviction, but revealed that he, alone among the ships' commanders, had questioned in a signal to the flagship the
distance specified between the columns and, after the collision, had offered to take in tow the *Victoria* as a last
desperate measure to get her ashore before she went down.

Only Noel of the *Nile* possessed the courage, or the
necessary conviction, to give direct evidence against Markham, if "only with great reluctance." "My hope was up to
the last moment that he would not turn," he said; and
later, when asked by Culme-Seymour, at the request of
Markham, whether "it was still in the power of the First

Division to circle round the Second?" he replied: "Yes, but it was equally in the power of the Second Division to turn away."

This was the strongest and most direct blow Markham had yet received—"an observation," according to the *Standard,* reporting the feeling in Malta that night, "which has given rise to considerable comment." It was also one which, on the following day, Markham attempted unsuccessfully to have expunged from the minutes of the court.

Markham made only one more appearance before the court, and that on the last day of the trial. Culme-Seymour was anxious to clear up one last point about the events on the *Camperdown*'s bridge. Had the rear admiral cancelled the order to semaphore the flagship querying the signal to turn, before or after Tryon had demanded, also by semaphore: "What are you waiting for?" Markham claimed that it was Tryon's impatient demand that had decided him to carry out the order without further delay. But his flag lieutenant denied this, saying that the signal had not been reported to Markham before he ordered the helm to be put over, and repeated his denial when recalled before the court. What had Markham to say about that?

"My reason for stopping the semaphore was because the semaphore signalled from the Commander-in-Chief was reported to me. I said by the Flag-Lieutenant, and I thought it was by the Flag-Lieutenant, and I think now it was by the Flag-Lieutenant. It was certainly reported to me by somebody. . . ."

The court adjourned at 2:15 on the ninth day of the trial to allow the chief defendant time to prepare his defence on the following morning. Captain Bourke retired with his papers. Rear Admiral Markham returned to his flagship with Captain Johnstone. The other officers and men, and the members of the court, were taken ashore for the last time. While Vice-Admiral Culme-Seymour, Commander John Jellicoe, Captain Winsloe, and Lieutenant Freemantle, the officer of the court, headed for the playing courts, where, in spite of the heat which had continued without a break for the entire hearing, they "made up a four at racquets for an hour's sweat."

The impressions that remained in the memories of all those concerned with the *Victoria* court martial before the reassembly, on those July mornings at Malta, were of the relentless midsummer heat that sapped a man of his vigour and drenched him within minutes of changing his clothes; the brilliant white of the buildings and great forts of the harbour—a dazzling strip dividing the clear blue of the sky from the clear, still blue of the water; and the bulky old wooden hull of the *Hibernia,* faintly intimidating, the little gigs and steam pinnaces, whalers, and other boats scurrying from shore to her gang ladders like anxious servants. On that last morning these impressions were heightened by the sense of expectation caused by the solemnity of the occasion and by the knowledge of the power wielded by the officers of the court. Nothing new was expected from Captain Bourke's defence, and a verdict of not guilty was generally anticipated; but the court was at liberty to comment on the conduct of the *Camperdown*'s officers, and even to cause the convening of a new court martial at which Markham might be accused of ramming and sinking the fleet's flagship.

It seemed, indeed, faintly inappropriate that it should be Captain Bourke, rather than Markham, who should be standing bareheaded before Culme-Seymour and the members of the court, his officers behind him, the 250 seamen in the roped-off area they had occupied on the first day of the trial, still guarded by armed bluejackets. It was twenty minutes to eleven when he started to read from his papers the text of his defence, speaking, according to the *Globe*'s report, "in a clear, loud voice, amid breathless silence, the whole scene being an intensely dramatic one."

"Gentlemen," he began, "in placing before you the defence of the surviving officers and men on their trial for the loss of H.M. Ship *Victoria,* I would first express to you, and to the service in general, with what true and sincere feelings we one and all tender our thanks for the very great sympathy and kindness which has been shown to us on all sides. Everyone seems to have striven to lighten our sorrow and help us in our distress. . . ." With the conclusion of this obviously sincerely felt expression, the first reference to Tryon could not be long deferred. Bourke's evidence had shown that he held, however reluctantly, his commander-in-chief responsible for the order that had led to the disaster. It only remained now to see if he had anything new to add, and to see how he intended to clear himself of responsibility at the expense of the reputation of his revered late admiral, who was unable himself to offer any defence. It was a delicate task.

"In manœuvres of any sort, the Commander-in-Chief, except to discuss as to the actual position of anchoring, never consulted anyone as to the manœuvres he intended to carry out. I even think that the Flag-Lieutenant very seldom knew any intention of the Admiral until the moment of the signal. I do not say this to lead the Court to suppose that I for an instant think I ought to have been consulted. The Commander-in-Chief was always ready and glad to discuss any manœuvre after it had been performed, but I never knew him to consult anyone before. . . . I must say I think any impressions I did have arose from my absolute faith and confidence in the Commander-in-Chief. . . . I would add, I think that no one ever criticized the Commander-in-Chief as to what he intended to do. I do not know to what extent I may go, but I do not seem to think that open criticism to one's superior is quite consonant with true discipline. . . .

"Sir George Tryon had a master mind. He loved argument, but was a strict disciplinarian. He always used to say he hated people who agreed with him, but that again was different from arguing against a direct order. With this and the fact that I was serving under an Admiral whose experience was far reaching, and whose vast knowledge of the subject of manœuvre was admitted by all, I seem to have left his cabin not clear in my mind what was to happen, but confident somehow that the Commander-in-Chief himself must be clear as to his intentions."

Bourke went on to describe once again, in considerable detail, the events that occurred and the action that was taken on board the *Victoria* before and after the collision. He continued to read in the flat, clipped tones with which the court had become so familiar over the past ten days, until he described the moments before the ship capsized. He had to pause several times to collect himself as he gave special credit to "those who, to the end, remained below stolidly, yet boldly, at their place of duty. All honour to them especially." And then on deck, where "it only wanted two or three to start a panic, but I think it should be on record that not one was found who had not that control over himself which characterizes true discipline and order."

A few moments later the emotional tension in the court-room was further heightened when reference was made to the lost midshipmen. "There is one deeply sad circumstance connected with the accident, and that is the very large pro-portion of midshipmen who lost their lives," Bourke managed to read, only with the greatest difficulty. He then broke down completely, the hand holding his papers falling to his side, and his head lowered, it might have been in prayer or because he was too moved to speak. Before he continued, sobs were heard from many parts of the court-room and, as one reporter told his readers, "All present were deeply touched and there were few dry eyes."

"These young officers at the commencement of their career were thus cut off, but it will be to their undying honour that, young as they were, they also showed the spirit of trust and bravery, and one and all remained at their posts on deck to the end."

A generous acknowledgement to Tryon, and the defence was concluded.

It was all over. Before eleven o'clock the court had been cleared, and the members retired to deliberate with Culme-Seymour until luncheon. The poop deck of the *Hibernia* remained empty except for a party of bluejackets, who swept down the deck and arranged the furniture, until two o'clock, when the court reassembled in private.

Then at seven minutes past three the court bell was rung, and once again, for the last time, the great body of prisoners was escorted in, silent in anxiety, followed by the prosecutor, witnesses, and audience. In front of Culme-Seymour lay the shining sword, and not one in the assembly of nearly five hundred packed under the awnings commented on its position with the hilt towards Bourke.

"The Court finds," began the deputy judge advocate when there was complete silence, "that the loss of Her Majesty's Ship *Victoria,* off Tripoli, on the coast of Syria, on the twenty-second of June, 1893, was caused by a collision with Her Majesty's Ship *Camperdown,* and it is with the deepest sorrow and regret that the Court further finds that this collision was due to an order given by the then C.-in-C., the late Vice-Admiral Sir George Tryon, to the two divisions in which the Fleet was formed to turn to sixteen points inwards, the leaders first and the others in succession, the columns at that time being only six cables apart.

"Secondly, the Court finds that after the collision had occurred everything that was possible was done on board Her Majesty's Ship *Victoria* and in the squadron generally both to save life and to save the *Victoria,* and the Court is of opinion that the order given by the late Vice-Admiral Sir George Tryon to annul sending boats, but to hold them in readiness, was, under the circumstances, a wise one.

"Thirdly, the Court finds that no blame is attributable to Captain the Honourable Maurice Archibald Bourke, or to any other of the surviving officers and the ship's company of Her Majesty's Ship *Victoria,* for the loss of the ship; and therefore it acquits them accordingly. The Court desires to record its opinion that the discipline and order maintained on board the *Victoria* to the last by everyone was in the highest degree creditable to all concerned.

"Fourthly, the Court feels strongly that, although it is much to be regretted that Rear-Admiral Albert Hastings Markham did not carry out his first intention to semaphore to the Commander-in-Chief his doubt as to the signal, it would be fatal to the best interests of the Service to say he was to blame for carrying out the directions of his Commander-in-Chief, present in person.

"Fifthly, the Court has placed in the Minutes all the evidence obtainable with regard to the closing, or otherwise, of the watertight doors of Her Majesty's Ship *Victoria*, but it does not feel itself called upon, nor does it consider itself competent, to express an opinion as to the cause of the capsizing of the *Victoria*."

Admiral Culme-Seymour rose from his seat, tall and gaunt and spendid in the dignity and power his braid and epaulettes conferred on him, and lifted Bourke's sword by the blade.

"Captain Bourke," he said, "I have very much pleasure in returning you your sword. The Court is dissolved."

10

A good deal has been said of late as to freedom being
given to inferiors to question and disobey the orders
of a superior officer. Discipline must be the law, and
must prevail. It is better to go wrong according to
orders than to go wrong in opposition to orders.

The Duke of Cambridge addressing
Woolwich cadets, August 1893

THE MEMBERS OF THE COURT had accomplished a most
difficult feat. No verdict could have wholly allayed the
anxieties and answered the criticism of the nation; but to
find that only the late commander-in-chief was to blame,
that the behaviour of the officers and men of the *Victoria*
was beyond criticism, and that even Rear Admiral Markham was guilty only of hesitancy in questioning his commander-in-chief's orders, seemed to be as satisfactory as
could be expected and in the best interests of the service.
Again someone had blundered, and the *Victoria*'s noble six
hundred had kept true to the traditions of Balaclava. There,
for a time, the matter rested officially, and Markham continued his appointment as second-in-command of the
Mediterranean Fleet under Sir Michael Culme-Seymour,
leaving Malta on the *Trafalgar* in the middle of August
"with much relief."

There was no faction in the service prepared to suggest,
even privately, that Tryon's order had not been the chief
cause of the catastrophe. Nor was it considered that there
had been any possible interpretation of the signal other

than the one Markham had accepted and executed, or that of turning inwards, to reverse the order of the fleet. But there were some among the younger "new generation" of officers, whose influence was out of proportion to their rank and numbers, who were astonished at the leniency that had been shown to Markham and the officers of the *Camperdown.*

Markham was by no means the most popular flag officer in the Navy, and the lack of initiative and control he had shown on June 22, and the equivocal yet defiant attitude he had taken at the court martial, offended some of these ambitious new career officers. The rear admiral, they felt, was no more than a burden to the service, and the sooner he was retired the better. It was "all nonsense," wrote Admiral Sir Charles Dundas, that Markham was obliged to obey the signal. "He had no earthly excuse for mastheading his answering pendant. . . . He went blindly into the danger zone as soon as the flagship hauled down the signal." Of Tryon, Jackie Fisher wrote privately to Lord Spencer, at a time when our likeliest enemy was across the Channel, "Had he lived he would certainly have beaten the French." But the brilliant, boisterous, straight-talking young captain, who was to be most responsible for wiping away the cobwebs and creating the new Navy of 1914, and who already had the ear of their Lordships, had this to say of the *Camperdown*'s senior officers: "If I were Markham or Johnstone, but more especially the former, I never could hold up my head again." And a week later, in another letter to the Secretary of the Admiralty, he added: "I am very strongly of the opinion that the Admiralty should publicly share the regret of the Court Martial in regard to

Markham's action, and thus avoid any encouragement of the idea that an Admiral's second-in-command is to be an automaton."[1]

The decision to end the career of a flag officer who had, in effect, been acquitted by court martial, was a difficult one to take, and the manner of carrying it out had to be carefully considered. The course their Lordships eventually took, and one which Markham, with some justice, described as "unfair" and "illogical," was to issue an Admiralty minute on October 28, just four weeks after Fisher's letter to Lord Spencer. Markham was given no prior notice of this minute, nor was he officially informed of its publication. He read about it eventually in an old copy of *The Times* while cruising in the Levant late in November.

In emphasizing again Markham's hesitancy and lack of initiative, the Sea Lords of the Admiralty made clear to all naval officers, if only by implication, their intention never again to employ him in a seagoing post of any responsibility. The minute confirmed the findings of the court, and went on, "Their Lordships concur in the feeling expressed by the Court that it is much to be regretted that Rear-Admiral A. H. Markham did not carry out his first intention of semaphoring to the Commander-in-Chief his doubts as to the signal: but they deem it necessary to point out that the Rear-Admiral's belief that the Commander-in-Chief would circle round him was not justified by the proper interpretation of the signal." The lack of "promptitude and decision" shown by Captain Johnstone, who "did

---

[1] *Fear God and Dread Nought, the correspondence of Admiral of the Fleet Lord Fisher of Kilverstone,* edited by Arthur J. Marder (London: Jonathan Cape, 1956).

not even order extreme helm to be used" or "carry out the orders which he had received with due rapidity and efficiency" was also referred to; and their Lordships felt bound "to express regret that he did not manifest the promptitude and decision which the occasion demanded for the security of his ship."

As Commander R. T. Gould wrote,[1] the *Camperdown* was "neither a smart ship nor very competently handled." That fact was made clear, if only by implication, at the court martial, even though attention was not drawn to the fact that the ship's second-in-command was below decks during the crucial manœuvre, that the starboard telegraph was not manned and that the ship's captain had made a vital alteration (about the time of the order to close watertight doors and to call the crew to collision stations) in the ship's log. Almost every decision and every action taken on board the *Camperdown* was either inept or badly carried out. But it is still difficult to defend the highly unusual and faintly underhand method their Lordships resorted to, except perhaps in terms of the nation's peace of mind. For the public to be told three months after the court martial that not only the commander-in-chief, but also his second-in-command, had been guilty of a blunder, would certainly have reopened controversy and might have caused political repercussions in the Admiralty. The *Victoria* disaster had lost the Navy some of the new confidence that the country had begun to show in the service, and already it was feared that the 1894 estimates might be in danger. To ruin his reputation privately was the most judicious and most expedient way of dealing with a discredited flag officer.

[1] *Enigmas* (1946).

In Malta the verdict of the court martial was "received with the greatest satisfaction," according to *The Times;* and there were many among the "old brigade" in the Admiralty and home-based establishments—those who had been brought up on sail, on spit-and-polish and form, on the traditionalism of nearly a hundred years of peaceful security—who were unable to conceal their satisfaction that Sir George Tryon's loose manœuvring and signalling principles had been proved impractical and dangerous and their disturbing influence removed. The disaster confirmed that the old ways were the best ways, that there were no short cuts in the conduct of a fleet, and that the Mediterranean Squadron's dangerous and deplorable T.A. System was finished; although these same officers, like Markham, always denied that T.A. had been in effect at the time of the collision. Chief among these was Captain P. H. Colomb, an arrogant and pompous theoretician, who had been responsible for the drawing up of the Royal Navy's system of tactics as long before as 1865 (since when few revisions had apparently been required), and had fought relentlessly against Tryon's simplified T.A. System. In a long letter to *The Times* a few days after the end of the court martial, he could afford to be condescending to Tryon. "The whole Navy will recognize my unique position with regard to all that relates to fleet manœuvring," Colomb modestly opened his three-column letter, "and any conclusions I arrive at . . . must have behind them a considerable mass of knowledge." To one officer, at least, the cause of the collision was clear. It was Tryon's dislike of "exact experiment," especially with regard to turning circles or manœuvres. Colomb deplored Tryon's disregard of "those exact intimations by signal of the Admiral's intentions which had been from time immemorial held to be necessary." And of Tryon's short-cut methods: "From the little I have been able to gather regarding the T.A. System, it does not appear to me that it could have produced the gain in time that it was credited with." If the captain had been able to gather only little about the TA system, it was because he could not have bothered to read the full memorandum on "A System of Fleet Manœuvres with and without Signals" which had been circulated throughout the Mediterranean Squadron and the Admiralty nearly two years before and had created something of a furore; nor could he have read any of the subsequent memoranda which, among other advantages, proved that messages from the flag to the ships of a squadron could be transmitted four times more quickly than by the traditional method.

This letter merely gave public expression to the general opinion of the conservative clique. The significant thing is that not one among the new generation, to whom Tryon had been the adored prophet, would publicly come to the support of his reputation. Only Captain Noel protested in *The Times* at Colomb's use—no less than four times—of the term "poor Sir George Tryon"; and he got into serious trouble with their Lordships for doing so. "In what way is he poor?" Noel demanded. "And what naval officer—worthy of the name—would not give anything they possess to be considered so great and rich in accomplishment as our late beloved Commander-in-Chief?"

Privately, Jackie Fisher wrote, "I have always held that Tryon was right in so many of the manœuvres he practised, and even in this last fatal one, as bringing about sudden, unusual, and difficult movements to exercise his captains for war exigencies." It was the nearest anyone in the service could bring himself to hinting that Tryon had not been wholly in the wrong. "Even in this last fatal one . . ." But no one else was to read that pregnant phrase for sixty years, until Fisher's correspondence was published.[1]

But Sir George Tryon's place and reputation in naval history were firmly established by the findings of the court martial, the urgent necessity of pinning the blame on to one man whose "master mind had fatally erred," and the popular outcry against him for sending 350 innocent bluejackets to a watery grave. Nothing could have saved his reputation, and the most charitable (and often repeated) conclusion that appropriately summed up the opinions of naval correspondents, editorial writers, and numerous sea-dogs in their memoirs, was *humanum est errare*. There the case has rested. But is there no defence that Sir George Tryon might have been able to put forward if he had not gone to the bottom, caught up in the rigging that netted in the *Victoria*'s chart-house roof? Is it not possible that his signal was capable of another interpretation, one that Markham certainly did not recognize, and one that the other captains present were at least not willing afterwards to admit they had recognized?

Tryon wanted to reverse the direction of his two columns but retain their relative positions, and afterwards to turn them 90 degrees to port to their anchorage. His signal specified only that the ships were to turn in succession and that the order of the fleet was to be preserved. The order of the fleet was: the *Camperdown* and *Victoria*, at the heads of the two divisions, the *Camperdown* to port of the *Vic-*

[1] Marder.

toria. Therefore, when the reversal of direction had been carried out, the *Camperdown* had still to be on the port beam of the *Victoria*. This could be accomplished only by the *Victoria*'s leading the first division round the *Camperdown* and the second division, as Markham had interpreted the signal; or by the *Victoria*'s taking the first division *inside* the turn of the *Camperdown* and the second division. The evolution could have been carried out only by one of these two methods, for if the two divisions had turned in towards each other, the second division would have then been to starboard instead of to port of the first division, and the order of the fleet would not have been preserved.

The all-important fact that the signal specified that the order of the fleet was to be preserved was omitted from the findings of the court martial, from the account of the collision in Brassey's *Naval Annual* for 1894, from the records in official and contemporary journals, and even from the standard biography of Sir George Tryon. No one in the Navy appears to have regarded the phrase as of importance, although its meaning was clearly defined and understood by every naval officer.

Tryon was as aware as the humblest midshipman in his fleet that two battleships could not turn safely towards each other at a distance of six cables, and he also knew that eight cables would have resulted in the fleet's re-forming in single line-ahead, and would have been almost as dangerous unless screws were reversed, a procedure he would not countenance on manœuvres except in an emergency. At least ten cables were necessary. He was, at first, not greatly concerned as to whether it was six or eight cables, as he revealed by his first acceptance of Hawkins-Smith's plea that it should be eight. But it is possible that, when he recognized that the slower-witted and conservative Hawkins-Smith had misinterpreted his plans for the evolution, Tryon, with a certain maliciousness, decided to order the narrower distance between the two columns, characteristically without explaining his plan, and emphasizing his decision by writing the figure "6" on a slip of paper. Hawkins-Smith and the others would understand later why, for the accomplishment of his intentions, the distance was of no importance. But, when his order was queried a second time, it was also in character that Tryon should show his annoyance. Time and again those who served under him had told of Tryon's refusal ever to discuss his plans before a manœuvre —and of his readiness to discuss them afterwards.

Rear Admiral Markham, however, did belatedly recognize that in order to preserve the order of the fleet one column would have to turn inside the other. His plea was that he thought the *Victoria* was going to circle round him. But why should Tryon not have intended the *Camperdown*, with its division following "in succession," to circle round the *Victoria?* This theory was put forward by only one authority (and he was not in the service), William Laird Clowes, in a letter to *The Times* of July 5, 1893, who supported it by quoting Queen's Regulations, Chapter 27, Sections 15 and 16: "If two ships under steam are crossing so as to involve risk of collision, the ship which has the other on her starboard side shall keep out of the way of the other."[1]

There were more arguments to support this theory that Tryon was ordering perhaps an unorthodox but certainly a safe and feasible manœuvre. At the court martial Lord

---

[1] The argument was subsequently enlarged and developed in his *History of the Royal Navy* (1903).

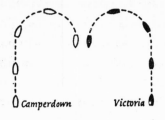

1.

The "impossible" manœuvre Tryon was commonly supposed to have attempted.

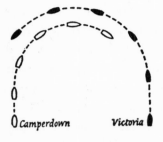

2.

The manœuvre Markham supposed Tryon intended.

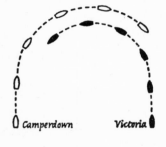

3.

The manœuvre as Tryon may have intended it.

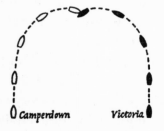

4.

The manœuvre as it was carried out.

THE FATAL MANŒUVRE

Gillford had confirmed that the T.A. system might have been in effect on that date, quoting Tryon as saying that "ships are constantly under the influence of T.A." Tryon was therefore justified in making a signal that left much to the judgement of his subordinates, whose actions were governed by the movements and helm signals of the flagship. The *Victoria* was at once put over at full helm, and Markham in the *Camperdown* was able to observe this from the flagship's helm signals. Indeed, he claimed, "I watched very attentively the helm signals," although this did not prompt him to ease the helm of the *Camperdown* to permit the *Victoria* to turn inside him. And, as Clowes maintained, "there is a well-recognized naval custom which dictates that a subordinate shall give precedence to a Commander-in-Chief, and shall not cross his bows without permission, but shall go under his stern."

One of the most damning pieces of evidence produced against Tryon by the old school was that this particular evolution had never been carried out before in the Mediterranean Fleet and was not even recognized by the official manœuvring book. This was perfectly true. But many evolutions not illustrated by diagrams in the official book were carried out in both the Channel and Mediterranean Squadrons. This identical signal was hoisted under rather different circumstances three times in one morning by Captain Noel with the second division when he was in temporary command of it earlier in the year; and again, under identical circumstances, in the Channel Fleet under Lord Charles Beresford in July 1908. It was unorthodox but recognized. In fact, it was not only recognized but actually provided for in Vice-Admiral W. F. Martin's standard work on manœuvring entitled *Observations on*

Steam Tactics, a book in which "it is proposed to furnish principles by which to conduct the ordinary evolutions of a steam fleet at sea." Accompanied by a diagram, it directed that "with respect to changing the 'Formation bearings' of a squadron in more than one column, suppose the alteration of Formation bearing to be 16 points . . .[1] let the port column . . . pass outside the starboard. . . ." Nobody publicly referred to these clearly stated instructions either at the court martial or, officially or unofficially, in print after it. But Tryon might reasonably have expected his subordinates to read official documents issued by the Admiralty.

It does appear, therefore, that there are at least some grounds for believing that, if Tryon had been given the opportunity to defend himself, he might have been able to justify both his signal and the course of action he followed. "As my commanders will testify," he might have said, "all my manœuvring orders were designed to exercise the initiative of my second-in-command and my subordinates. It is the whole purpose of fleet evolutions to test and to train the powers and intelligence of officers."

Then was Sir George Tryon made the scapegoat for reasons of convenience and expediency? It must be accepted that strong evidence in his favour was withheld or understated before, during, and after the court martial. There can also be no doubt that, both officially and unofficially, efforts were successfully made to cast doubts on Tryon's general reputation and on his behaviour on the fatal afternoon. It was common talk in clubland, for example, that he was drunk after a heavy lunch, and that there was nothing unusual about this. When this theory was later put

---

[1] As it was on this occasion.

forward by a tactless guest at a dinner party at which Lord Gillford was present, Tryon's former flag lieutenant was so outraged that he lost his temper and stormed from the room. The highly respected and influential Admiral Hornby wrote in the *United Service Magazine* (August 1893) that Tryon was still suffering from a bout of Malta fever, and therefore not in full control of his senses. "I have no doubt that he was so suffering and gave his orders in complete forgetfulness"; although Fleet Surgeon Ellis, who had been attending him daily, had testified at the court martial that he was in perfect health and had not even suffered from fever. Numerous remarks were made at the court martial, none of which may have been intended to cast a slur on the C.-in-C., but which certainly succeeded in doing so: Bourke's testimony that he had spoken "rather shortly"; the suggestion that he had been in such a daze, and with his eyes averted from the approaching *Camperdown*, that he had failed three times to hear his captain's appeal to reverse the screws, although there was a good deal of outside noise at the time and he was hard of hearing in one ear, and it later developed that Tryon always kept his eyes astern at the crucial moments during evolutions, which naturally required concentration; the frequently repeated testimony that he had called off the boats, that it was left to subordinates to give the order to abandon ship and, later, the *sauve qui peut*. Then there was the confidential memorandum dispatched to Lord Rosebery for the information of the Cabinet by his friend Lieutenant-Colonel Trotter, who was present on the occasion. This not only emphasized that Tryon had called off the boats ("an order which sent a chill through my veins") but included a detailed diagram of the anchoring formation which, by naming each ship in the fleet in its intended position, served to prove that Tryon must have intended the columns to turn in on each other. In fact, the positions which each ship should take up were never specified by Tryon, only that they were to anchor in columns of divisions line abreast to port.[1]

There is nothing to show that there was any conscious malevolence behind any of this evidence, least of all in the evidence of Tryon's own subordinates, but there would be a strong, natural, and justifiable sense of self-protection among defendants and witnesses alike. This is not to suggest that there was any form of conspiracy; and no doubt the silent service lived up to its reputation for discretion.

All this must forever remain as supposition. No one will ever know for sure what Tryon's intentions were when he gave the order which resulted in the sinking of the *Victoria*. Individual theories can start and end with the possible interpretations of those five words he spoke on the chart house, which were heard by two officers of undoubted integrity, and can be accepted as the truth. "It was all my fault," he said. Did Sir George Tryon mean, "It was all my fault. I have made an appalling miscalculation and this is the result?" Or did he mean, "Markham is a greater fool than I had imagined him to be. But now that my ship is to sink and many of my men are to die, I shall die with them and it is better that I should take the blame?" Or is the true interpretation something between these two ex-

---

1 It has frequently been argued that only by turning the columns inwards towards each other, and so reversing the bearings of the flagships, could Tryon have brought the *Victoria* to its recognized position, nearest to the land and to the landing-place (see map, p. 129). But Tryon was not of a nature to allow such a practice to interfere with one of his evolutions.

tremes? Did he perhaps mean, "I have still not succeeded in instilling sufficient initiative, intelligence, or imagination into my second-in-command. I have again overestimated his powers, this time fatally, and, as supreme commander, I am therefore entirely to blame"?

Or was Tryon perhaps more strongly affected than he revealed by Markham's deficiencies, and, in contrast to his own obsessive single-mindedness, by Markham's apparent indifference to fleet manœuvring? And, as a result, did some kind of unconscious antagonism towards his second-in-command blind Tryon to the realities of the situation, even though these were pointed out to him at least three times? No one will ever know. It is too late to discover the truth now; and it was too late to discover the truth on June 22, 1893. Even those present at the time, even the men closest to the two admirals, like the members of the court martial and the theoreticians and historians ever since, could only conjecture.

EPILOGUE

Having attained command of the greatest single naval force in the world, George Tryon had set himself the task of transforming it from a tradition-bound team of display men, unsurpassed at the ritualistic performance of standard evolutions, at brass-polishing, everyday seamanship, and elaborate signalling, to an imaginative, sharp-thinking, and daring fighting team. Tryon's belief was that his fleet must be ready for war, rather than for peaceful exhibitionism; and whether he was right or wrong on the afternoon of June 22, 1893, he died striving to complete his task. It was fortunate for Britain that great men like Fisher, who succeeded him in the higher councils, were bred in the same tradition. The *Victoria-Camperdown* affair immediately preceded the reorganization of the administration of the Royal Navy, from the signalling branch to the construction department, brought about by the arms race with Germany and the threat of war in Europe. Within a very short time the firmly entrenched Victorian principles of tactics, manœuvring, gunnery, and signals which had applied in 1893 were to become as obsolete as the mixed-armament, heterogeneous ironclads Tryon had commanded.

Many of those present at the catastrophe, such as Jellicoe, Noel, and Wilson, went on to achieve the highest distinctions and honours in the Royal Navy. But few of the *Victoria*'s officers personally involved in the fate of the two flagships survived for long; it was almost as if they too had been condemned by that Syrian fakir's prophecy. Hawkins-Smith died within a few years; Bourke died of consumption in 1900; Lord Gillford five years later at the age of thirty-seven. But Markham lived longer, growing more taciturn and embittered as he recognized how completely his career had been broken and how forgotten he had become. He was allowed to serve out the last few months of his appointment as second-in-command, Mediterranean. He then went on to half-pay and devoted much of his time to Freemasonry, a society to which he had been loyal for some years. At least he achieved distinction in the Masonic world, becoming the Grand Master for Malta, and later the Founder and the First Master of the Navy Lodge. But, apart from a term as commander-in-chief of the Nore, Markham received little further encouragement from the Admiralty, and finally retired in 1906. The offer of his services was refused during the Boer War and in 1914, when he worked in the capacity of Treasurer of the Minesweepers' Fund. At the age of fifty-three he married a stolid Scots woman, Theodora Gervers. She was many years younger than Markham, bore him a daughter, and provided him with much solace during his last years. Markham never recovered from the distress and shame of the *Victoria* collision, which killed even his old love of exploration and travel. He died a fortnight before the end of World War I, on October 29, 1918, shortly after completing his last book, the eulogistic biography of his cousin Clements.

The fate of Sir George Tryon's beloved T.A., and of all the vessels that exercised under this system in the summer of 1893, was equally sombre. T.A. died, discredited, with its creator; but its end was only a little premature, for within six years the first wireless telegraphy equipment to be fitted to a battleship was being used on manœuvres, and long before 1914 "the T.A. system" was only a term among the curiosities of nineteenth-century naval history. Of the *Nile,* the *Dreadnought,* the *Inflexible,* and the others, none present off the Tripoli coast that afternoon was thought worthy to be kept even in the reserve by the time World War I was imminent. All were relegated to guardship duties within five years. The *Camperdown* alone had a longer life, avoiding the demotion to guard duties until she went to Lough Swilly in 1900.

Paradoxically, it was the *Victoria* herself which attracted the greatest attention, even a morbid interest, long after the collision. Her tantalizing proximity to the shore, her mere ship's-length from the surface, fascinated many people and exercised the ingenuity of hundreds of amateur inventors, who thought either that the taxpayer could be saved three-quarters of a million pounds, or that there was quick salvage money to be made. Over a hundred plans for locating and raising the *Victoria* were received by the Admiralty from various eccentric inventors, and even from some reputable firms. Some of the applicants wanted £50,000 ($250,000) on the nail and £250,000 ($1,250,000) on delivery, some said they would do it for patriotic reasons, using a "submarine steamer" or a diving bell; one wanted to drag the wreck into shallow water, another to bring it up through a tube, using rubber bands to protect the hull. But none of these offers was accepted by the Admiralty, and not even a diver descended to explore the *Victoria*'s secrets. She lies today, broken and mud-shrouded, with her monster 111-ton guns, with her entombed admiral and bluejackets, on the bed of the Mediterranean.

SOME SOURCES CONSULTED

BOOKS

An Admiral Yarns: Stray Memories of 50 Years, by Admiral Sir Charles Dundas of Dundas (1922)

Memories of a Bluejacket, 1872–1918, by Patrick Riley (1927)

My Naval Career, 1880–1928, by Admiral Sir Sydney Robert Freemantle (1949)

A Naval Scrapbook, 1877–1900, by Admiral Sir Reginald H. Bacon (1925)

The Story of a Naval Life, by Admiral Sir Hugh Tweedie (1939)

Admiral Jellicoe, by Arthur Applin (1915)

The Life of John Rushworth Earl Jellicoe, by Admiral Sir Reginald H. Bacon (1936)

Mysteries of the Sea, by J. G. Lockhart (1924)

Memories of a Marine, by Major-General Sir George Aston (1919)

The Navy in My Time, by Admiral Mark Kerr (1933)

Famous Shipwrecks, by Frank H. Shaw (1930)

The Life of Sir Albert Hastings Markham, by M. E. and F. A. Markham (1927)

The Life of Admiral Sir George Tryon, by Admiral C. C. Penrose Fitzgerald (1897)

Naval Recollections, 1852–1914, by "A Retired Flag Officer" (Admiral Sir N. Bowden-Smith) (1914)

Admiral of the Fleet Sir Geoffrey Phipps Hornby, by Mrs. Fred Egerton (1896)

My Memories, by Grand Admiral von Tirpitz (1919)

Naval Memories and Traditions, by Admiral Sir Herbert King-Hall (1926)

A Great Seaman: The Life of Admiral of the Fleet Sir Henry F. Oliver, by Admiral Sir William James (1956)

Battleships in Action, by R. W. Wilson (1926)

British Naval Policy, 1880–1905, by Arthur J. Marder (1940)

The Nation and the Navy, by Christopher Lloyd (1954)

A Short History of the Royal Navy, by Christopher Lloyd (1942)

Steamships and their Story, by R. A. Fletcher (1910)

Fear God and Dread Nought: The Correspondence of Admiral of the Fleet Lord Fisher of Kilverstone, selected and edited by Arthur J. Marder (Vol. II, 1956)

British Battleships, 1860–1950, by Oscar Parkes (1957)

Memories, by Admiral of the Fleet Lord Fisher of Kilverstone (1919)

A Rough Record, by Admiral Sir William Goodenough (1943)

Sea Fights and Shipwrecks, by Hanson W. Baldwin (1956)

Enigmas, by R. T. Gould (1946)

The History of the Royal Navy, Vol. VII, by Sir William Laird Clowes (1903)

Dictionary of National Biography

NEWSPAPERS

The Times. The Standard. The Globe. The Manchester Guardian. The Morning Post. The Daily Graphic. The Daily News. The Daily Mail. The New York Times. The New York Tribune.

PERIODICALS

Nature. The Graphic. The Illustrated London News. The Navy. The United Services Magazine. The Army and Navy Gazette. Proceedings of the United States Naval Institute. Journal of the Royal United States Services Institution. The Saturday Review.

OTHER SOURCES

Brassey's Naval Annual. Navy Lists. The Noel Papers in the National Maritime Museum. Ships' Logs and Signal Logs and Naval Dispatches 1892–93. Proceedings of the Court Martial of the Captain, Officers and Men of H.M.S. *Victoria.*